THE YEAR OF LUKE

bringing home the Gospel

A
WEEKLY
JOURNAL
FOR
CATHOLIC
PARENTS

Judith Dunlap

ST. ANTHONY MESSENGER PRESS
Cincinnati, Ohio

Scripture passages have been taken from the *New Revised Standard Version Bible,* copyright ©1989 by the Division of Christian Education of the National Council of the Churches of Christ in the U.S.A., and used by permission. All rights reserved.

Cover and book design by Mark Sullivan

LIBRARY OF CONGRESS CATALOGING-IN-PUBLICATION DATA

Dunlap, Judith.
Bringing home the gospel : a weekly journal for Catholic parents : year of Luke / Judith Dunlap.
p. cm.
Includes bibliographical references and index.
ISBN-13: 978-0-86716-782-5 (pbk. : alk. paper)
ISBN-10: 0-86716-782-3 (pbk. : alk. paper)
1. Bible. N.T. Luke—Devotional literature. 2. Spiritual journals—Authorship. 3. Church year meditations. 4. Family—Religious life. I. Title.
BS2595.54.D86 2006
242'.645—dc22

2006017559

ISBN-13: 978-0-86716-782-5

ISBN-10: 0-86716-782-3

Published by St. Anthony Messenger Press
28 W. Liberty St.
Cincinnati, OH 45202
www.AmericanCatholic.org

Printed in the United States of America.

Printed on acid-free paper.

06 07 08 09 10 5 4 3 2 1

• DEDICATION •

For my husband Roger, and my children Roger, Kristin, James, Phillip and Peter—for their patience and love as I learn to let go. I am so proud of all of you.

For the wonderful women who listened, counseled and mothered me through my early years of mothering: Ann Armstrong, Mary Mayeres, Susan McDonald, and most especially my mother Ann Zcelinski and sisters Janice and Joyce.

• CONTENTS •

Introduction ..... *vii*

Journaling With the Scriptures *1*

Six Traits of Strong Families *5*

Following the Church Year *9*

Liturgical Calendar: Year of Luke *13*

Liturgical Journal *15*
   Advent *15*
   Christmastime *23*
   Ordinary Time *29*
   Lent *89*
   Easter *101*

Extra Journal Space *123*

In my adult life I kept one daily journal, and that was only sporadically for two months. I recently came across the book, and as I read the pages I wished I had somehow found the time and willpower to have kept on writing. (Perhaps a weekly diary might have worked for me.)

I had three children under six and was nine months' pregnant with our fourth child when I started writing in the journal. I have no idea how I found the time or why I began, but I am certainly glad I did.

That winter was cold and snowy, and we had just moved to a new city. My husband was working twelve hours a day almost seven days a week, and I didn't know anyone. The journal entries read like a cross between Charles Dickens and *The Brady Bunch* without Alice.

When I found the journal, I discovered how much I had forgotten from those early family days. I had forgotten that the electricity was out when we brought our newborn home from the hospital—twenty-four hours without light, except for candles, and heat, except for the fireplace.

Four days before our son was born, I was using a plumber's snake to retrieve my husband's rolled-up socks from the toilet. While I was on my hands and knees in the bathroom, my two- and three-year-olds were busy coloring a life-sized mural of our family on their bedroom wall in crayon.

There are several journal entries where I find myself losing it, and wishing with all my heart I was worthy of the beautiful children God blessed me with. I kept telling God to be patient with me: I would get organized, and I would gain control. (You can read the reflection for the Fifth Sunday after Easter to find out how the situation finally was solved.)

I wish I had continued the journal so I could read about how I evolved from a stay-at-home mom to a working mom. I would particularly like to have had a record of when our fifth child was born, and when I came to realize that I would never be Carol Brady or any of those other TV supermoms who never lost their tempers or watched leftovers change colors in the refrigerator.

The journal has become one of my treasured keepsakes. Each time I read it I am taken back to that tiny house on St. Matthew Street, and I can reconnect with that young, struggling mom who tried so hard to be perfect. The added gift is that when I read the pages out loud, my adult children can go back with me and hear about those days—giving them a verbal picture of their early years that is so much more authentic than any photograph or video. I hope this journal offers you the same gift.

• JOURNALING WITH THE SCRIPTURES •

This weekly journal is meant for busy folks who are trying to raise spiritually healthy and well-balanced children, while staying spiritually healthy and well-balanced themselves. It is for parents who don't have time for a daily journal, but would like to keep a personal diary as well as a family record of the year. Each week you will find a reflection based on a Sunday Gospel. The readings are primarily from the Gospel of Saint Luke with a few from Saint John (Cycle C in the church's liturgical calendar).

This journal can be used in conjunction with the designated Sunday readings from the church calendar, or it can be picked up at any time during the year and used as a weekly journal. The Scripture passages follow the life of Jesus from his conception through his death and resurrection and are therefore easily adapted to your own schedule. However, if you would like to correlate your journal entries with the Gospels read at Sunday worship, make sure you read the "Following the Church Year" section beginning on page 9.

Using the Journal
Scripture Citation and Date
At the top of each week's page is the title of the Scripture passage. You will also find the citation telling you where you can find the passage in the Bible. Below the citation is a place for you to write the date. Above the title you will find the Sunday of the church year when this Gospel is read.

Scripture Reflection
The Scripture reflections were written especially for you as a parent. They are not meant to be a theological exegesis. They are

intended to do what a Sunday homily is supposed to do, which is help you bring the Word of God home and apply it to your life. These reflections will help you grow in your relationship with God so that you can become all that God created you to be—including the best-ever parent.

Family Response

The Family Response questions or suggestions are meant to give you an opportunity to talk with your children about God and the things that are important to your family. You are the person primarily responsible for the faith development of your child. If you want your child to believe in God and consider faith an important dimension of life, she needs to see that God is a reality in your life and that your faith is important to you.

If you are going to use Family Response, I suggest you find a comfortable spot in your home and let that be your regular gathering space for this family activity. You might light a candle and begin with a short prayer. Read or retell the week's Scripture passage out loud in your own words. Ask youngsters what they think the passage is about. Offer your own thoughts; feel free to adapt comments from the reflection for that reading. Finally, read the Family Response question or suggestion out loud. After everyone has had a chance to think about his or her answer, ask for responses. Make sure that you respond also. Consider ending with another short prayer.

You may, of course, make up your own Family Response, choose not to use the family piece every week or choose not to use it at all. Whatever the case, try to find time to read to your family from a good children's Bible, pray with them every day and, above all, talk to them about God. Let them know how much God loves them. Make sure they know that there is nothing they can do that would stop God from loving them.

Personal Response

The personal questions following the reflection are only suggestions. Feel free to adapt them (or ignore them) and include your own. If you need more writing space, there are additional pages in the back of the book; just mark your entry with the page number on which you continue. This is your journal. If the Gospel reading or the reflection touches you in a particular way, or if something significant is happening in your life, feel free to use the page to record or reflect on what is important to you at that time.

Last Week and Next Week

The last questions each week are always the same:

> "What do you want to remember from last week?"
> "What are you looking forward to next week?"
> "What are your concerns?"

Use this space for the generalities of family life *(We had four soccer games and teacher conferences…)* or the specific details of a particular day or event *(Tuesday was horrendous. First, I…)*. Write about your thoughts and feelings. I can pretty much assure you it will be these details you will most appreciate when you reread your journal years later.

I want to pass on to you the results of a survey I share with almost every parent group I speak with. Two researchers, Nick Stinnett and John DeFrain, from the University of Nebraska, Lincoln, conducted a study in which they surveyed three thousand families that were identified as "strong and healthy." These families came from a variety of ethnic, racial and economic backgrounds and represented both one- and two-parent households.

Stinnett and DeFrain discovered that strong families all share the same six traits. These traits did not come naturally to the families. They flow from "deliberate intention and practice." As you read though the weekly reflections, you will find that I occasionally refer to the following familial characteristics:

Committed

Strong families are committed to being a *family* first and foremost. Like many families, strong families are busy and overextended, but strong and healthy families are committed to making one another a top priority. The members of these families disagree, argue and are sometimes even guilty of infidelity. But strong families recognize that overcoming a crisis is often the catalyst that leads to making an even firmer commitment to each other. Commitment takes sacrifice and an unselfish attitude. Commitment can be seen as the "hinge quality" upon which the other qualities hang.

Affirming

All people need affirmation, and strong families are aware of this. Its members make a point of noticing the little things that others do around the house. They celebrate one another's achievements. Most importantly, they not only affirm one another for what they do but also for who they are.

Together

Strong families, no matter how busy, find time to spend together. They eat, play and work together. They do not buy into the old "quality not quantity" adage. Strong families are present—and spend both quality and quantity time together. Even if it means sitting down and scheduling family time, strong families find time for each other.

Communicative

Strong families communicate well and often. Members are willing to share their thoughts and opinions about what is happening in each of their lives. Each member is willing to share his or her feelings. Good communication also involves accepting another's feelings and listening without interruption.

Helpful and Flexible

All families have problems, and—let's face it—some of us have big problems. Strong families are flexible. They learn to bend, not break, in a crisis. They don't let problems fester. They deal with them as soon as possible. They know when to go for outside help. Strong families do not lay blame, but work together to resolve the situation. They discover that going through hard times can make individuals as well as the family itself stronger.

FAITH

Strong families have a healthy spirituality. They believe in a higher power that can transform their lives and offer hope and purpose. Strong families pray together, and find that their shared faith helps to form a strong family bond. (I found this last trait rather surprising, considering that the study was done by a secular institution. The survey showed that while not all strong families belong to an organized religion—although the majority did—they all consider themselves highly faithful or religious.)

C.A.T.C.H. FAITH

There is an easy way to remember these six traits—a simple phrase using the first letter of the first five qualities—*C.A.T.C.H.* followed by the sixth word, *faith*. And that is precisely how it happens. Young people cannot be preached or beseeched into faith. It is something they can only catch from being around others who have an active faith life of their own.

You are the most important person in the faith development of your child. No church, no school, no religious education program can compare to the influence you have on your child's faith life. Give your children the gifts that will last a lifetime: love, hope and a living faith.

• Following the Church Year •

The Sunday readings are meant to inspire us to live our lives as God's children. They invite us to bring peace and harmony to our homes and to a world that sorely needs it. The readings also offer us hope to keep us going week after week. This book offers you the opportunity to continue reflecting on the Gospel by bringing the Word home with you from Sunday liturgy. If you choose to use the journal by following the Sunday readings, the information that follows will be helpful.

What Is the Liturgical (Church) Year?

Calendars have been used for thousands of years to mark time as well as the seasons. Our common calendar is divided into four equal seasons: winter, spring, summer and fall. Our church, or liturgical, calendar also has four seasons, but each season is a different length, and some are separated by a varied number of weeks designated as Ordinary Time.

The church calendar revolves around two great events: the Incarnation (Christmas) and the Resurrection (Easter). Each of these celebrations is preceded by a season of preparation and anticipation (four weeks of Advent before Christmas, and six weeks of Lent before Easter). They are each followed by another season of celebration and thanksgiving (the twelve days of the Christmas season and the seven weeks of the Easter season). Weeks of Ordinary Time separate these seasons. During Ordinary Time we celebrate the everyday experience of Christ in our lives.

The church year begins on the First Sunday of Advent. The number of Ordinary Sundays varies each year depending on which major feast days fall on Sunday.

Lent begins with Ash Wednesday, midweek before the first Sunday of Lent. You will find a calendar with the dates marking the seasons and Ordinary Time on pages 13–14.

The Sunday readings follow a three-year cycle using a different Gospel each year: Matthew is used for year one, Cycle A; Mark for year two, Cycle B; and Luke for the third year, Cycle C. Readings from John's Gospel are used throughout the three-year cycle, particularly during the Easter season. The book you have in your hands is based on the readings from Saint Luke, Cycle C. If you are interested, you can go to page 12 to see what years are in which cycles.

When to Begin?

It's always best to begin at the beginning, and for a journal based on the church year that would be on the First Sunday of Advent. However, if you purchase or receive this book sometime after Advent, you can still use it to follow the Sunday readings of the church year.

If you begin in January, I would suggest you start with the Christmas reading sometime before the first Sunday. That way you can follow the life of Jesus from the beginning.

If you begin this journal midyear, check page 13 to learn where to begin to write in the book. Sometime in November, Cycle C will end. If you wish to continue following the church year, you will need to begin a new weekly journal for Cycle A on the First Sunday of Advent.

Remember, you can always choose to use this weekly journal independent of the Sunday readings at church. Just begin with the first reading and follow the life of Jesus in your own time and on your own schedule.

The Lenten and Easter Seasons

Since this journal is not designed for a specific year, the pages do not always follow in the chronological order of a church year. The book begins in Advent followed by the Christmas season, all of the Sundays in Ordinary Time and, finally, Lent and Easter. Since Easter is celebrated on different Sundays each year, the number of Sundays in Ordinary Time between the Christmas season and Lent will vary. This means the reader must leave Ordinary Time and turn to page 89 for the First Sunday of Lent. (This will usually follow the Sixth, Seventh or Eighth Sunday in Ordinary Time.) After the Easter season, the reader will return to the next Sunday in Ordinary Time.

Please Note:

• You will notice that this journal has fifty-four weeks, two more weeks than the common calendar or our church calendar. The additional entries are Christmas and the Baptism of the Lord, both important events in the Jesus story. When following the church calendar, I would suggest reading the reflections on the actual feast day or sometime in the middle of the week. Alter the reflection questions if it seems appropriate.

• During Lent there are sometimes two sets of readings, one to use if your parish is involved in the Rite of Christian Initiation of Adults (RCIA) process, another if the parish is not involved. Since most parishes are engaged in the RCIA, this book uses those particular readings.

• When important feast days fall on a Sunday, the Scripture read at Sunday worship will be different from the Gospel reading found in this journal. Again, since this book was not written for a specific year, it was decided to keep the usual readings for the Year of Luke.

Example of a Ten-Year Lectionary Cycle
(2006-2016)

Year	Lectionary Cycle
December 2006–November 2007	C (Luke)
December 2007–November 2008	A (Matthew)
December 2008–November 2009	B (Mark)
December 2009–November 2010	C (Luke)
December 2010–November 2011	A (Matthew)
December 2011–November 2012	B (Mark)
December 2012–November 2013	C (Luke)
December 2013–November 2014	A (Matthew)
December 2014–November 2015	B (Mark)
December 2015–November 2016	C (Luke)

LITURGICAL CALENDAR:
YEAR OF LUKE

Sunday or Feast Day	2007	2010	2013
First Sunday of Advent	12/03/06	11/29/09	12/02/12
Second Sunday of Advent	12/10/06	12/06/09	12/09/12
Third Sunday of Advent	12/17/06	12/13/09	12/16/12
Fourth Sunday of Advent	12/24/06	12/20/09	12/23/12
Christmas, December 25	Monday	Friday	Tuesday
Holy Family	12/31/06	12/27/09	12/30/12
Epiphany	01/08/07	01/03/10	01/06/13
Second Sunday in Ordinary Time	1/14	1/17	1/20
Third Sunday in Ordinary Time	1/21	1/24	1/27
Fourth Sunday in Ordinary Time	1/28	1/31	2/3
Fifth Sunday in Ordinary Time	2/4	2/7	2/10
Sixth Sunday in Ordinary Time	2/11	2/14	—
Seventh Sunday in Ordinary Time	2/18	—	—
Eighth Sunday in Ordinary Time	—	—	—
Ninth Sunday in Ordinary Time	—	—	—
First Sunday in Lent	2/25	2/21	2/17

Sundays in Lent follow in order

Easter Sunday	4/8	4/4	3/31
Second Sunday of Easter	4/15	4/11	4/7

Third through Seventh Sundays of Easter follow in order

Pentecost	5/27	5/23	5/19
Trinity Sunday	6/3	5/30	5/26
Body and Blood of Christ (Corpus Christi)	6/10	6/6	6/2
Ninth Sunday in Ordinary Time	—	—	—

	2007	2010	2013
Tenth Sunday in Ordinary Time	—	—	6/9
Eleventh Sunday in Ordinary Time	6/17	6/13	6/16
Twelfth Sunday in Ordinary Time	—	6/20	6/23
Birth of John the Baptist	6/24	—	—
Thirteenth Sunday in Ordinary Time	7/1	6/27	6/30

Fourteenth through Nineteenth Sundays in Ordinary Time follow in order

	2007	2010	2013
Twentieth Sunday in Ordinary Time	8/19	—	8/18

Twenty-first through Thirty-third Sundays in Ordinary Time follow in order

	2007	2010	2013
Thirty-third Sunday in Ordinary Time	11/18	11/14	11/17
Christ the King	11/25	11/21	11/24

• LITURGICAL JOURNAL •

ADVENT

Don't Be Anxious

This Gospel from Luke is read on the first Sunday of Advent, the season we are to prepare for the coming of Jesus, not just as a baby but also at the end of time. It's a frightening reading about roaring seas and nations in disarray. Jesus tells his disciples to pray for the strength to stand firm, "Be alert at all times, praying that you may have the strength to escape all these things that will take place, and to stand before the Son of Man" (v. 36).

My generation worries, as did generations before, about how quickly the world is changing. We've watched technological development escalate. We see the global scope of poverty and the rising horrors of terrorism and genocide. We live in an age of constant alteration and altercation, and we are worried.

> **First Sunday of Advent**
> *Luke 21:25–28, 34–36*
> date: ___ / ___ / ___

Parents today are responsible for preparing children for a future none of us can even imagine. We have no idea what questions or decisions today's children will face. Yet somehow, in the few precious years from infancy to adulthood, parents must equip their youngsters with the tools that will help them not only survive, but also do well, while revitalizing the world they inherit.

Certainly one of the key factors in facing the uncertainties of the future is belief in a greater reality, and hope in a higher power.

> **"Be alert at all times, praying that you may have the strength to escape all these things that will take place, and to stand before the Son of Man" (v. 36).**

So much is possible and bearable when you believe in a loving God who promises not only to be *with* you but also *in* you. So much is possible and bearable when you know you are a part of something that is true and good, bigger and stronger than our chaotic world. So much is possible and bearable when you know you are not alone and can count on the support of others who will be there for you and with you. These are important truths in an uncertain world—important for grown-ups, too.

Family Response: Ask each person to share the best thing that happened to him or her this week. What was most difficult?

Personal Response: As you begin this journal, what are your hopes and concerns for the year ahead?

_____

_____

_____

_____

_____

What were the highlights from last year?

_____

_____

_____

_____

_____

What are you looking forward to next week? What are your concerns?

_____

_____

_____

_____

John the Baptist Prepares the Way

John the Baptist, Jesus' cousin, was a prophet who came to prepare the people for Jesus. John was a holy man who spent most of his time praying in the desert. When he left the desert, he traveled throughout the region of the Jordan calling people to repent and change their lives: "Prepare the way of the Lord, make his paths straight" (v. 4).

God calls each of us to a close, intimate relationship. Toddlers and teens, grown-ups and elders are all invited to share in God's love. The invitation is extended in all sorts of ways: through Scripture and study; through friends, relatives and acquaintances; in quiet spaces and noisy places.

Second Sunday in Advent

Luke 3:1–6

date: ___ / ___ / ___

But God especially counts on parents to issue the invitation to children, to introduce them to a loving God and to nurture their relationship with Jesus Christ. Our church baptizes infants because we trust that children will be nourished by their parents' faith until they are old enough to claim their own.

"Prepare the way of the Lord, make his paths straight" (v. 4).

Like John the Baptist, parents are expected to prepare the way so their children will be open to accepting God's personal invitation.

This can be done in subtle ways, such as creating a Christian environment at home with crucifixes and Bibles or beginning family rituals, such as nightly prayer or seasonal devotions (such as praying together around an Advent wreath).

But the most effective way for children to know who God is and what God asks of them is by listening to and watching the people who are most important to them.

If God is going to be a reality in their lives, children must see in actions and hear in words that God is a reality in the lives of their mothers and fathers. For children, God's invitation to a forever relationship is best delivered personally through the words and example of their parents.

Family Response: Ask each family member to find something in the house that makes him or her think about God or faith. Talk about what each person finds.

Personal Response: Are you comfortable talking about your faith with your family? Why or why not?

_____

_____

_____

_____

_____

What do you want to remember from last week? What are you looking forward to next week? What are your concerns?

_____

_____

_____

_____

_____

John the Baptist Baptizes With Water

John the Baptist prepares the way for Jesus by telling people to repent. He baptizes them with water as a sign of their repentance. When people begin to think that John might be the Messiah, he makes it very clear that they are wrong. He tells them that one mightier than he is coming. "He will baptize you with the Holy Spirit and fire" (v. 16).

When John the Baptist's followers are ready to turn away from their dishonesty and selfishness, he baptizes them with water, a cleansing ritual that signifies their wish to repent. But repentance is not enough to bring freedom and salvation. It takes the Holy Spirit and the new life Jesus offers us through his life, death and resurrection.

> *Third Sunday of Advent*
> *Luke 3:10–18*
> *date: ___ / ___ / ___*

> **"He will baptize you with the Holy Spirit and fire"**
> **(v. 16).**

Repenting, or saying we are sorry, is the first step to freedom and salvation. The second step is to focus on changing our behavior. If we say we are sorry and have no intention of changing our actions, we can't be forgiven. Even God cannot free us from sin if we insist on holding on to it. Sometimes we are really sorry for our actions but can't muster the courage to change. In that case, we need to ask God for the *desire* to change. Even this small inclination to mend our ways is enough to loosen sin's grip and allow the Holy Spirit to slip in.

The third step is to admit we need help. We humbly acknowledge that we need God's help to love the way God wants us to love. We face our limitations and even our powerlessness, and ask the Spirit to fill us with strength and new life. We trust that with God's help we can overcome our sins or our most compelling bad habits and become the person God calls us to be.

Family Response: Adult family members may want to practice a simple Act of Contrition using the three steps above. (*Say you are sorry. Promise to change. Ask for God's help to do better.*) Say this prayer with your children before bedtime.

Personal Response: What about yourself would you like to change? What keeps you from changing? Are you ready to ask for God's help to change?

_____

_____

_____

_____

_____

_____

_____

_____

_____

What do you want to remember from last week? What are you looking forward to next week? What are your concerns?

_____

_____

_____

_____

_____

_____

_____

_____

Mary Visits Elizabeth

Mary is pregnant when she sets off to help her cousin Elizabeth, who is also pregnant. Mary has just said "yes" to becoming the mother of Jesus. Elizabeth welcomes Mary, and experiences a special blessing for herself and her child. She praises Mary for her faith and rejoices with her over her miracle.

Mary was newly pregnant and not married when she left for Judah. She probably spent much of the journey wondering how her cousin would receive her. Imagine her relief when she saw Elizabeth's face and heard her greeting: "Blessed are you among women, and blessed is the fruit of your womb."

Sometimes we forget that Mary was just a young girl, probably about fourteen, when she agreed to become the mother of Jesus. There is no questioning her courage and colossal faith, but she was probably still confused and scared after the angel left.

Mary came to help her cousin, but (as is often the case) she ended up being ministered to also. How affirming it must have been to hear Elizabeth, an older woman, praise her for her faith and trust in the Lord. Like all of us, Mary needed to know that she was not alone. Her courage and faith needed to be bolstered. Elizabeth gave Mary the reinforcement she needed.

Fourth Sunday in Advent
Luke 1:39–45
date: ___ / ___ / ___

"And blessed is she who believed that there would be a fulfillment of what was spoken to her by the Lord" (v. 45).

Like Mary, we are also asked to have faith and to believe in the promises of a God we cannot see. We are asked to believe in God's unconditional love for us, and to say "yes" to that love so that like

Mary we too can bring Jesus into the world. Amidst all our confusion and fear, God asks us to have the courage to share our faith, bolster the faith of those closest to us and make the presence of Jesus real in our households.

Family Response: Ask family members to talk about the last time someone bolstered their courage. Who are the people in your lives who remind you of Jesus? In what way?

Personal Response: Who are the people who remind you of Jesus? In what ways?

_____

_____

_____

_____

_____

_____

What do you want to remember from last week?

_____

_____

_____

_____

_____

What are you looking forward to next week? What are your concerns?

_____

_____

_____

_____

_____

CHRISTMASTIME

Jesus Is Born

In John's Gospel there is no account of Jesus' birth. Instead, John reminds us that Jesus has been a reality since the beginning, even before creation. Jesus is the Word who was with God and was God. Father, Son and Spirit are not sequential. They are One. The Word became flesh, he brought new life and this life was a light shining in the darkness. "The true light, which enlightens everyone, was coming into the world" (v. 9).

On the first Christmas a child was born who would change the world forever. He brought strength to the weak, courage to the fearful, consolation to the sad and hope to the abandoned. The child was Jesus. He brought light into the darkness.

All through the New Testament, and especially in John's Gospel, we hear Jesus referred to as "the light." We can understand this metaphor when we contrast the gift of light to darkness. Nothing changes when the lights go out, but in the dark we feel disoriented and vulnerable, sometimes even afraid. Turn on the lights, and we regain our sense of place and position. This is precisely why Jesus came.

When the world was created, it was good. There was harmony in the universe and a sense of peace in that harmony. When people were created, they were created good. Scripture tells us

> *Christmas Day*
> *John 1:1–18*
> date: ___ / ___ /___

> "The true light, which enlightens everyone, was coming into the world" (v. 9).

that humans were created in the likeness and image of God. With their Creator they shared the ability to love and to create good out of love. Somewhere along the way this was forgotten, evil moved in, and the lights went out. Disorientation, vulnerability and fear followed. Love became tarnished, and what humans designed was not always good.

And then came the first Christmas, and a new light came into the world. As John tells us in his Gospel, those who accepted the light were given the power to become the children of God. They regained their sense of place and position. The darkness had no power over them. They knew who they were and whose they were. Christmas celebrates this light, this life born in Bethlehem, with us still today and yet to come in glory.

Family Response: Share the Christmas traditions you remember from when you were growing up. Ask family members to talk about their favorite family Christmas traditions.

Personal Response: What are the positive things you want to remember about the family you grew up with?

_____

_____

_____

What do you want to remember from last week?

_____

_____

_____

What are you looking forward to next week? What are your concerns?

_____

_____

_____

The Holy Family

Jesus lived a rather ordinary life with his family. We have only one story from his childhood: Luke's account of Jesus being left behind in Jerusalem. I love this story because it makes the Holy Family seem so human, and it reminds us that even the holiest of families have problems.

Mary and Joseph are coming back from Jerusalem in a large caravan of relatives. After traveling for a full day they realize Jesus is missing. Imagine the scene. They are scared to death. Maybe they even argue a bit about what to do. Perhaps Joseph allows his fear to sound like anger as he questions Mary about when she has last seen Jesus. They turn around and retrace their steps to and through Jerusalem.

For three days they search for Jesus, concerned that he is afraid, alone and lost. Instead, they find Jesus in the temple, sitting comfortably with the teachers. Their relief turns to the very human emotion of frustration, as Mary asks her son, "Why have you done this to us?" Jesus answers like any other twelve-year-old: "I thought you'd know…."

Feast of the Holy Family
Luke 2:41–52
date: ___ / ___ / ___

"His mother treasured all these things in her heart" (v. 51).

Like all families, the Holy Family probably had times when their communication was less than perfect. Like all strong families, they probably said their "sorrys" and learned from their mistakes. I jokingly like to say that we don't hear about Jesus for the next eighteen years because he was grounded, but I'm just projecting a mother's frustration. More seriously, we know this was an important event for Mary, because she kept it forever in her heart.

Family Response: All families have problems. Handling problems in a positive way, and not letting them dissolve family unity, is a trait of strong families. And so is good communication. Ask family members to talk about positive ways of solving problems.

Personal Response: All parents hold things in their hearts regarding their children. What are the really special things about your child or children that you do not want to forget?

_____

_____

_____

_____

_____

_____

What do you want to remember from last week?

_____

_____

_____

_____

_____

What are you looking forward to next week? What are your concerns?

_____

_____

_____

_____

_____

Epiphany of the Lord

Wise men from the East have followed a star from its rising to find the new king of the Jews. They encounter a jealous Herod, the current king, who tries to have them reveal the child's whereabouts so he can get rid of him. When they find Jesus, they give him gifts of gold, frankincense and myrrh.

When the wise men find what they are looking for, they share their most precious treasures. What are *you* looking for? What is *your* most precious treasure?

You may not want to admit it, but if you are like most people, you have probably spent a great deal of your life hoping to find the love you deserve: a love that accepts and affirms you completely. Some people follow star after star, looking for that unconditional love, only to be disappointed over and over again.

Why does this happen? We are human, which is to say imperfect. At some point, all parents end up hurting and disappointing their children. Those hurts and disappointments condition the way we love. We become frustrated and lose our tempers. We push too much or say too much. We are jealous or too sensitive. And we find ourselves hurting and disappointing the ones we love most. Those who love us do the same.

If we are lucky, we find a spouse who will grow with us through those hurts and disappointments, and the love that blessed us when we were married grows and matures. And if we

> *Feast of the Epiphany*
> *Matthew 2:1–12*
> date: ___ / ___ / ___

> **"Then, opening their treasure chests, they offered him gifts of gold, frankincense, and myrrh"**
> **(v. 11).**

are really lucky, our children forgive us for the hurts and disappointments we inflicted on them, and they love us for a lifetime. But we poor, flawed humans can never love unconditionally in this lifetime.

The only way to find that love is to follow the same star the wise men followed: the star that leads to Jesus. Only God can love us unconditionally, and Jesus is the Way to God's love. Open yourself to God's love so that you can share that love with all its acceptance and affirmation with your most precious treasure: your children.

Family Response: It is important to affirm your children. Tell each family member what you like most about him or her. Ask other family members to do the same.

Personal Response: Where are you in your relationship with God? Are you open to discovering who God is and how much you are loved? If so, how can you go about it?

What do you want to remember from last week?

What are you looking forward next week? What are your concerns?

ORDINARY TIME

Jesus Is Baptized by John

John the Baptist tells his followers that he baptizes with water but that one mightier than he will baptize with the Spirit. John baptizes Jesus, and while Jesus is praying a voice is heard from heaven. "You are my Son, the Beloved; with you I am well pleased" (v. 21).

I think that Jesus, from the time he was very little, experienced the loving intimacy of being God's son. Because he was fully human, he probably assumed everyone else had the same experience. When he is baptized, he is not surprised by the voice calling him the beloved son. But perhaps he is surprised at the spectators' astonishment. This is the moment when Jesus finally understands that everyone else does not experience God as a loving Father as he does.

First Sunday in Ordinary Time
Luke 3:15–16, 21–23
date: ___ / ___ / ___

"You are my Son, the Beloved; with you I am well pleased" (v. 21).

After his baptism Jesus goes into the desert for forty days to pray about what he has discovered. He is tempted to use this knowledge for his own gain, but instead, he leaves the desert to begin his ministry. The rest of his life is spent trying to convince others—that includes us—that we are all are sons and daughters of God; a God who loves us unconditionally as the best-ever Father would. Remember the prayer Jesus gives his followers begins, "Our Father…". Everything else Jesus teaches follows from this.

If we open ourselves to God's love and allow that love to forgive our sins and heal our hurts, we begin to experience our kinship with God and all peoples. When we really believe that we are a son or daughter of God, we begin to see how precious and valuable we are. Because we are loved unselfishly, we can then love selflessly. And like our brother Jesus, we can become healers and peacemakers. And God's plan (sometimes called God's kingdom or reign) of justice, peace and harmony can become a reality in our lives.

Family Response: Talk to your children about how much God loves them. Do this often. Let them know how much you love them, and then tell them that God loves them even more. Ask them how they know God loves them. Tell them how you know God loves you.

Personal Response: Hear the words that were spoken when Jesus was baptized as if God is speaking them to you: "You are my beloved son or daughter. With you I am well pleased." Put those words in the first person ("I am God's beloved child"), and say them to yourself often. How does this make you feel?

_____

_____

_____

What do you want to remember from last week?

_____

_____

_____

What are you looking forward to next week? What are your concerns?

_____

_____

_____

Jesus' First Miracle: The Wedding Feast at Cana
Jesus and his friends attend a wedding in the town of Cana. When the wine gave out, the mother of Jesus said to him, "They have no wine" (v. 3). At his mother's request Jesus turns water into wine, thus sparing the host the humiliation of running out of wine. This is Jesus' first miracle—a miracle that went unnoticed except for Jesus' friends, his mother and the servers.

Even Jesus needed a gentle push from his mother to embark on his mission. When she mentions the problem of the wine, Jesus tells her it isn't his time yet. Mary, ignoring his protest, instructs the servers to do whatever he tells them. She knows her son. After all, she raised him, and she taught him the virtue of compassion.

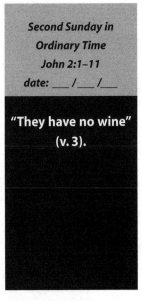

Second Sunday in Ordinary Time
John 2:1–11
date: ___ / ___ / ___

"They have no wine"
(v. 3).

I don't often think of Jesus as a child, but when I do I have to remind myself that he was a regular little boy. We know he never sinned, but if he was human he must have made mistakes. Like all good parents, Jesus' mother and father had to teach him to face his problems, deal with them and, if possible, fix them. It's obvious from this story of the wedding at Cana that they also taught him to be aware of other people's problems too.

Compassion, caring about others, is an essential quality for Christians. Help your children notice the little things: to see when their sibling or friend needs help. Open their eyes to the details of life. Help them develop empathy for those who are hurting, including the unspoken hurts of frustration, embarrassment, humiliation or defeat. Teach them to ask themselves: How would I feel? What can I do? Answer those questions with them when they are young.

Jesus' first miracle happened at a party because his mother pointed out that someone was in need. There was no big fanfare, no huge audience. Jesus responded, as he knew he should, as his parents had taught him. And his public ministry was launched.

Family Response: Have each family member name a talent that each other family member has. The same talent cannot be named more than once.

Personal Response: Compassion is feeling the pain of another. Acting compassionately is doing something in a positive way about it. How compassionate are you? Think of something that happened this week where you showed (or could have shown) your compassion.

_____

_____

_____

_____

What do you want to remember from last week?

_____

_____

_____

_____

What are you looking forward to next week? What are your concerns?

_____

_____

_____

_____

Jesus Teaches in the Synagogue

When Jesus entered the synagogue in Nazareth, the town in which he grew up, he was handed a scroll of Isaiah and invited to read. He began,

"The spirit of the Lord is upon me,
because he has anointed me
to bring good news to the poor.
He has sent me to proclaim release to the captives…" (v.18).

Jesus had left the desert following his baptism. He was feeling great. He had faced his temptations and was eager to begin his ministry. He went to the synagogue to pray. Imagine his surprise when he was given this particular Scripture to read. The words spoke to his experience. He was aware that the spirit of God was upon him. He felt he had been anointed to bring wonderfully good news wherever he went.

> **Third Sunday in Ordinary Time**
> Luke 4:14–21
> *date:* ___ / ___ / ___
>
> **"The spirit of the Lord is upon me, because he has anointed me to bring good news to the poor. He has sent me to proclaim release to the captives…" (v.18).**

The words from Isaiah must have confirmed for Jesus what he had discerned in the desert: He had a mission that would eventually be shared by all those who truly came to know him. On that day in the synagogue in his hometown of Nazareth, Jesus takes Isaiah's words and proclaims them as his own. He will open the eyes of those who cannot see and work his whole life to free those who are oppressed.

Jesus is aware that many people can see the trees but be blind to the forest. He knows that someone can be held captive and still walk freely in the world. His mission is to open people's eyes to God's love so they can love in the same way. His mission is to free those who are oppressed by fear and loneliness as well as greed and prejudice.

Jesus invites all people to be a part of the kingdom of God, and to bring justice to those who are poor, suffering and physically oppressed. He gave his life in faithfulness to this mission, and he offers us the same invitation. Through his life, death and resurrection, Jesus has freed us from oppression if we are willing to open ourselves to the new life he offers.

Family Response: Ask family members to talk about one thing they are afraid of. Talk about why they think they have that fear.

Personal Response: What are some of your fears? Do they hold you back? Do they keep you from being the best you can be? Are you willing to let go of those fears by asking for God's help?

_____

_____

_____

_____

What do you want to remember from last week?

_____

_____

_____

_____

What are you looking forward to next week? What are your concerns?

_____

_____

_____

_____

Jesus Is Rejected in Nazareth

After Jesus reads the passage from Isaiah, he tells those listening, "Today those words are fulfilled in your hearing." The people are shocked at his apparent audacity. After all, they *know* him. They watched him grow up. He is just a carpenter's son. In their fury they drive Jesus out of town. "Truly I tell you, no prophet is accepted in the prophet's hometown" (v. 24).

The people who have known Jesus the longest, and who should be his staunchest supporters, reject him. And Jesus' reply to them becomes a classic quote familiar to even non-Christians. The line, "a prophet is never accepted in his own place" is used today to refer to any person of ability who goes unappreciated by those who know him best.

Fourth Sunday in Ordinary Time
Luke 4:21–30
date: ___ / ___ / ___

"Truly I tell you, no prophet is accepted in the prophet's hometown" (v. 24).

As a mom, I have certainly felt that way. I remember a chocolate jellyroll ice cream cake I made for one of my sons' birthdays. It was covered in whipped cream and made to resemble a covered wagon complete with horses and little carved marshmallow people. My masterpiece was wolfed down in seconds without a single "wow" from the birthday boy, his siblings or his father.

I have also been on the other side of the equation and done my share of not appreciating family members. I'll make a point of telling a friend what a fine meal he has served, but forget to compliment my husband on his newest smoked sausage creation. It's even worse when I treat complete strangers better than I do my own family.

There have been times when I was in a really grumpy mood, and somehow managed to be pleasant to the cashier or even a stranger in the street. Yet when I came home, I'd find myself barking at my children. Today's reading from Luke reminds us to pay attention to how we treat those who are closest to us. We need to open our eyes and really see them—recognize their talents and efforts and appreciate them for the terrific people they are.

Family Response: Ask each family member to talk about a time when he did not feel appreciated. Have each person thank him or affirm him individually. Talk about ways you can show someone you appreciate him.

Personal Response: Here is your chance to get your gripes on paper. Do you feel you are not appreciated by your family or coworkers? In what ways? Are you as appreciative of your family or coworkers as you should be?

_____

_____

_____

_____

What do you want to remember from last week?

_____

_____

_____

_____

What are you looking forward to next week? What are your concerns?

_____

_____

_____

_____

Jesus Chooses His First Disciples

While Jesus is teaching, he notices two fishermen casting their nets and catching nothing. Jesus gets into one of the boats and tells the men to go into the deep water and lower their nets. Begrudgingly, the men row out, cast their nets and catch a great number of fish. Simon, James and John become Jesus' first disciples. "When they had brought their boats to shore, they left everything and followed him" (v. 11).

Imagine leaving everything behind to follow what you know is the right path. Jesus' apostles each made a commitment to be with him. Jesus became their number-one priority. The apostles all shared the same commitment and eventually formed a small community. It was a community strong enough to stay together, faithful to Jesus' message even after he died. Commitment makes a community strong. It does the same for a family.

Jesus was with his disciples almost daily for three years. They ate together, prayed together, worked together and, I'm sure, they had fun together. The more time they spent together, the closer they bonded.

> *Fifth Sunday in*
> *Ordinary Time*
> *Luke 5:1–11*
> *date: ___ / ___ / ___*

> "When they had brought their boats to shore, they left everything and followed him" (v. 11).

Commitment to family involves the same activities. It takes eating, praying, playing and working with each other on a regular basis to build strong relationships. We have to earn a living and clean the house. We may have to take care of an aging parent. But if our family is a priority, we will find the time to be together.

Sometimes that means sitting down each week and pulling out your appointment book or PDA. If necessary, suspend your child's bedtime by a half-hour. Give up sleeping in on a Saturday morning or take the kids out of school for lunch if that's the only time you can find, but plan time each week to be together. It's that important!

Family Response: Sit down together and set a date for the whole family to spend two hours together. Decide what you want to do, and commit to it.

Personal Response: Do you find yourself choosing other commitments over your family? If so, how can you change this situation? Is it possible to commit some time each day to your relationship with God? Even five minutes in the morning, or before you fall asleep, would be great.

_____

_____

_____

_____

_____

What do you want to remember from last week?

_____

_____

_____

_____

_____

What are you looking forward to next week? What are your concerns?

_____

_____

_____

_____

The Beatitudes

Jesus continues to share his message of hope and love. Crowds begin to gather as his reputation spreads throughout the countryside. In this reading we hear about those who are blessed and those who are not. In the language of the day, to be blessed was to be happy. The blessings are called the Beatitudes. "Blessed are you who are poor, for yours is the kingdom of God" (v. 20).

Every December I used to search for the perfect gift for each of my children—a gift that I was sure would light up their eyes on Christmas morning. Like every parent, I take great delight in seeing my children happy.

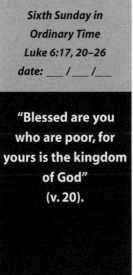

Sixth Sunday in Ordinary Time
Luke 6:17, 20–26
date: ___ /___ /___

"Blessed are you who are poor, for yours is the kingdom of God" (v. 20).

Imagine the satisfaction of being able to offer that joy with something that won't break when it's dropped or go out of fashion in a few months. That's the kind of happiness Jesus offers when he talks about the Beatitudes. Indeed, in his Sermon on the Plain, Jesus suggests we can be blessed with deep happiness in the most unpleasant of circumstances.

What's the secret of this joy, and how can we find it? We know it doesn't simply come with being poor or hungry, sad or persecuted. It might, however, be found in the way we look at and live through each of those situations.

Rich or poor, we all have to endure life's downs. No one can escape the pain of sickness or the death of a loved one. Perhaps the secret to happiness is in our accepting whatever life has to offer, certain that all will be well and confident of a happy ending.

All will be well because we don't have to rely solely on our own resources. God is with us, offering the strength we need. We also have the support of our family community in church and at home. And finally, we have the ultimate hope of a happy ending because Jesus has promised us one for eternity.

Family Response: Ask each family member to talk about his or her best family memory.

Personal Response: Have you ever experienced the kind of joy that can still bring a smile to your face today? What are the things that make you happy? Can you, or should you, make those things a regular part of your life?

_____

_____

_____

_____

_____

_____

What do you want to remember from last week?

_____

_____

_____

_____

_____

What are you looking forward to next week? What are your concerns?

_____

_____

_____

_____

_____

Jesus Tells Us to Love Our Enemies

Jesus continues to speak to the crowd, giving them perhaps his most difficult teaching. He tells them to give to everyone who asks and expect nothing in return. He instructs his listeners to love everyone, and reminds them that even sinners love those who love them. "…Love your enemies, do good to those who hate you" (v. 27).

This is the bottom line of what it means to be a Christian—loving even those who don't love you. However, it's important to understand what love really is. For example, you can love someone and not like him. Loving and liking are two different things. Love is a bond, sometimes accompanied by a warm and glorious feeling of devotion, even passion. But much of the time, love is just a strong sense of connection. The test for real love is when that wonderful, warm feeling is absent and the connection remains.

> *Seventh, Eighth &
> Ninth Sunday in
> Ordinary Time
> Luke 6:27–38*
> date: ___ / ___ / ___

> **"…Love your
> enemies, do good
> to those who
> hate you"
> (v. 27).**

This is the love Jesus is talking about—a loving bond that demands respect and tolerance. We are expected to recognize the connection that exists not just within our own families but also within the family of humankind, and to honor its demands. If someone chooses not to love us back, we do not allow her actions to dictate ours. We don't give others that power over us.

In your household when one brother smacks another, you don't persuade him to hit back. When one child is disrespectful of another's toys, you certainly don't encourage reciprocal action. All people are part of the family of humankind, and God, as a parent, offers the same advice you would give your children.

Teach your children by example. That's what God did. Jesus stood up for what he believed. He never cowered. But when things got too hot, he walked away, and usually found a quiet spot to pray and regroup. When he was ultimately overpowered and put to death, he still triumphed. That's the message of the Resurrection: The love God asks of us will always see us through. It is even more powerful than death.

Family Response: Ask family members to talk about someone they have trouble liking. Do not allow any belittling. Try to talk about the person in a respectful way. Finally, find at least two things that are nice about that person.

Personal Response: How do you usually treat people you do not like? How do you respond when someone is unkind to you? How would you like to respond?

_____

_____

_____

_____

_____

What do you want to remember from last week?

_____

_____

_____

_____

_____

What are you looking forward to next week? What are your concerns?

_____

_____

_____

_____

Jesus Forgives a Sinful Woman

Jesus is invited for dinner; when he arrives he is not honored with the customary hospitality of being kissed, or having his feet washed. While he is at table, a woman (a notorious sinner) approaches him and begins to wash his feet and kiss them. Her sorrow is so deep that her tears are used in the washing. The host berates Jesus for allowing this behavior, but Jesus is impressed with her sincerity.

Making children say the words "I forgive you" won't change the way they feel about someone who has hurt them. Helping them deal with those feelings is an important step in the complicated process of learning to forgive. We can teach them this life lesson in sit-down, eye-to-eye conversations. But the way they will really learn the process is by watching our everyday actions.

> *Tenth & Eleventh Sunday in Ordinary Time*
> Luke 7:36–50
> date: ___ / ___ / ___

> "…[H]er sins, which were many, have been forgiven; hence she has shown great love" (v. 47).

I was reminded of this simple truth when I was driving my four-year-old granddaughter home one day. When I asked Dana how things were going at preschool she told me how angry she was at her friend Maggie. I told her I was surprised, because I knew that Maggie was her best friend. "She still is," Dana explained. "Just because you're mad at somebody doesn't mean you don't still love her. Sometimes," she went on, "it just means you're frustrated."

I was amused by Dana's precocious response, but proud of her, too. My granddaughter was beginning the process of forgiving her friend by looking at her own reaction and feelings. She may have been simply repeating what Mom and Dad told her when they heard about her preschool experience, but I am also certain she was using the words she heard when her parents had reached their own frustration level.

Parents are wise to use every teachable moment to verbalize a message, but the spoken lesson is lost if Mom or Dad isn't willing to model it. Dana will likely continue to parrot her parents' words for some time, but if she continues to receive their loving support and witness their fine example, I have no doubt she will grow up to have a forgiving heart all on her own.

Family Response: Ask family members to talk about why it is difficult to forgive some people. Ask them to think about a time they themselves were forgiven. Talk about the incident and how they felt.

Personal Response: Is there someone you have difficulty forgiving? What would it take to make that happen? Are you willing to take any steps?

_____

_____

_____

_____

What do you want to remember about last week?

_____

_____

_____

What are you looking forward to next week? What are your concerns?

_____

_____

_____

Jesus Talks About Life, Death and Suffering
Jesus, alone with his disciples, begins to talk about life, death and
suffering. He knows that the prophets who challenged the
established order usually ended up dying for their beliefs. He did
not have to be God to know things would not go well for him. He
sees the same suffering ahead for his disciples, and encourages
them to accept the crosses they must endure.

We try so hard to shelter our children from harm's way. But
eventually there comes a day when we realize we can no longer
protect them from the crosses of an imperfect
world. Crosses are a part of the human condition.
Everyone has them. Jesus asks us to accept our
crosses and be graced through them—not to
bellyache or feel sorry for ourselves, but to pick
them up and carry them.

> *Twelfth Sunday in*
> *Ordinary Time*
> *Luke 9:18–24*
> *date: ___ / ___ /___*

> **"If any want to
> become my
> followers, let them
> deny themselves and
> take up their cross
> daily and follow me"
> (v. 23).**

When my oldest son was five, we moved into
a neighborhood of preschool bullies. Every
afternoon I sat on the porch and supervised. I
feared the day he would be on his own in
kindergarten. It finally dawned on me that
constantly shadowing his outdoor play wasn't
doing him any favors. At some point, I realized, he
needed to learn to take care of himself.

One sunny day in late August, after practicing
what to say and what to do, I sent him out by himself. When the
door shut behind him, I rushed to the window and peeked
through the curtains. Later, I wondered if this was how God felt
observing us. Was God like a deeply concerned mom, reluctantly

untying the apron strings, giving us our freedom with all the risks that come with it?

We teach our children how to do this by talking about our own crosses, helping them strategize ways of growing through their own and letting them know that we are there to listen and help in a pinch. Finally, we try to make sure they understand that God is always close by, peeking through the curtains, loving them through their hurts and, like us, ready to shoulder some of their burden.

Family Response: Ask family members to talk about something really difficult they had to get through last week. How did they handle it?

Personal Response: What are some of the crosses you are carrying right now? Do you feel that you are handling them well? How can you get help if you need it? How can your faith help you?

_____

_____

_____

_____

_____

What do you want to remember from last week?

_____

_____

_____

_____

What are you looking forward to next week? What are your concerns?

_____

_____

_____

_____

What It Takes to Be a Disciple

When Jesus and his disciples are turned away from a Samaritan village, the disciples want to send down fire to punish them. Jesus rebukes them and continues on the journey. As various people approach Jesus asking to be disciples, he points out the difficult choices they will have to make if they want to follow him. "No one who puts a hand to the plow and looks back is fit for the kingdom of God" (v. 62).

Our faith is not just a Sunday endeavor. Being a follower of Jesus is a lifetime, 24/7 commitment. It affects what we say, what we do and how we view the world. Being a Christian is not easy.

Thirteenth Sunday in Ordinary Time
Luke 9:51–62
date: ___ / ___ / ___

"No one who puts a hand to the plow and looks back is fit for the kingdom of God" (v. 62).

Christians don't distinguish between "them" and "us." They believe that all people are God's children, and are worthy of respect. Christians realize that a person's worth is not determined by how pleasant he or she is or by how much he or she is liked. Christians turn the other cheek. They don't plot revenge. Christians go out of their way to help anyone who crosses their path. They see every living person as their brother or sister. They see all of creation as gift to be appreciated and protected.

The job description can sometimes seem overwhelming. That is why we can take comfort in the way Jesus responded to his disciples when they wanted to destroy the city that refused them hospitality. God is very patient with us.

God is understanding, even when we fail or act most unchristian. God only asks us to make an effort each day, to ask for help when we need it and to say we are sorry when we mess up. One of the great lessons of being a Christian is accepting the fact that we cannot control everything. We will always need God's grace to strengthen us, heal us and work through us.

Family Response: Have each member talk about what he or she thinks it means to be a Christian. Is everyone living up to his or her own expectations of what they think being Christian means? What can each person do differently in his or her daily life to be more like Christ?

Personal Response: What is the most difficult part about being a Christian? Why do you think it is difficult? How can you make it easier?

_____

_____

_____

_____

_____

What do you want to remember from last week?

_____

_____

_____

_____

_____

What are you looking forward to next week? What are your concerns?

_____

_____

_____

_____

Jesus Sends His Disciples

Jesus appoints seventy-two disciples and sends them, along with
the apostles, into the various towns and villages. He tells them to
carry no money or sack, but to rely on the hospitality of the people
in the town. If they are welcomed in peace, they are to stay. If not,
Jesus tells them to leave. "…[T]he Lord appointed seventy others
and sent them on ahead of him in pairs…" (v. 1).

The disciples were going out to preach on their own. Jesus knew
the difficulties they would encounter, and so he sent them out in
pairs. This is a really important point. It is so much
easier to get things done, to manage difficult
situations or to even celebrate our
accomplishments with the help of others. We all
need support and encouragement. One of the
first things Jesus did when he began his public
ministry was to gather a group of people whom
we call *apostles* and *disciples*. Even Jesus needed a
community to walk with.

> **Fourteenth Sunday in
> Ordinary Time**
> *Luke 10:1–12, 17–20*
> date: ___ / ___ /___

> **"…[T]he Lord
> appointed seventy
> others and sent
> them on ahead of
> him in pairs…"
> (v. 1).**

This is why belonging to a church is so
important: Not just to have a group of people with
whom to worship, but also to have a community
to nurture and support you and your family. The
church community is asked to serve as a model
for us and our children; sometimes even offering
an alternate lifestyle to that of the culture in which we live. We need
to surround our children with people who share the same values.

Church is a family, and like every other family, the church is not
perfect. Every church makes mistakes, sometimes really big ones.

As we do in our family, we try to forgive and move on. Every church community will have its characters, its misfits and its sinners. We are not expected to like every member, but if we make an effort to get involved in church activities, we often meet people who can become surrogate family and lifelong friends.

Family Response: Ask family members what they like best about their parish. Who are some of their favorite people?

Personal Response: Is the parish community an important part of your life? If not, why? How can you become more involved? If you are involved, what are the fruits of your involvement?

_____

_____

_____

_____

_____

_____

What do you want to remember from last week?

_____

_____

_____

_____

_____

What are you looking forward to next week? What are your concerns?

_____

_____

_____

_____

_____

The Parable of the Good Samaritan

Jesus discusses the great commandment: to love God with your whole heart, soul and mind, and your neighbor as yourself. He is then asked the question, "And who is my neighbor?" (v. 29). Jesus answers with the parable of the Good Samaritan—the story of one man rescuing another. The rescuer belongs to a group of longtime adversaries of the Jews, the Samaritans. He helps a beaten man who was ignored by two of his countrymen. When Jesus finishes the story he asks, "Which of these three, do you think, was the neighbor to the man who fell into the hands of the robbers?" (v. 36).

Jesus answers his own question very clearly in this parable: Even the person you trust least is your neighbor. The Samaritan, despised by the Jews, helps a Jew. He goes out of his way to make sure the injured man is taken care of. The story is a testimony not only to who our neighbor is, but also to what it means to be a neighbor.

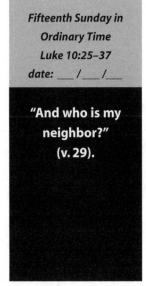

Fifteenth Sunday in Ordinary Time
Luke 10:25–37
date: ___ / ___ / ___

"And who is my neighbor?" (v. 29).

The Samaritan doesn't just stop to help the injured man; he carries him on his own animal to an inn where he leaves instructions with the innkeeper to take care of him. He even leaves enough money to pay for the injured man's needs, offering to pay any additional charges on his return.

This story reminds me of the illustration of a young boy carrying a smaller child on his shoulders, the sketch that accompanies the motto for Boys Town: "He ain't heavy; he's my brother." That is the lesson of the parable with the underlying awareness that we are all brothers and sisters.

When we see or even hear about someone in need, we are asked to put our own misgivings and prejudices aside and lift them up, just as the Samaritan did, just as the youngster commemorated in the illustration did, just as Christ is willing to do for us each time we fail or need to be carried.

Family Response: Go through a newspaper or a newsmagazine together and find pictures of people from another culture or country. Talk about what the picture tells you about the way they live. Imagine what it would be like to trade places with them.

Personal Response: Prejudice is something that is subtly passed from generation to generation. What prejudices did the family you grew up in have? Do you hold the same prejudices? How do you handle prejudice?

_____

_____

_____

_____

_____

What do you want to remember from last week?

_____

_____

_____

What are you looking forward to next week? What are your concerns?

_____

_____

_____

_____

Jesus Visits With Mary and Martha

When Jesus visits the home of his friends Mary, Martha and Lazarus, Mary sits at Jesus' feet listening to him. Her sister Martha is busy preparing dinner and serving it. When Martha complains that Mary is not helping, Jesus tells her that Mary is fine. "Mary has chosen the better part…" (v. 42).

Martha was right: Mary, a woman living in first-century Palestine, should have been up and about cooking and serving. But as in so many other instances, Jesus ignores the social norms of his times. He tells Martha, and all of us, that it is often more important to be a listener than a doer.

Sixteenth Sunday in Ordinary Time
Luke 10:38–42
date: ___ / ___ /___

"Mary has chosen the better part…" (v. 42).

Jesus wants us to be attentive to his presence, not only by spending time in prayer but also by recognizing him in the people we encounter, especially those in need. Unfortunately, we are sometimes so intent on getting the grass cut that we just give a wave to our out-of-work neighbor. Or we're so busy getting a late dinner cooked that we miss the opportunity to talk to an eight-year-old who is having a really bad day.

There are always a dozen things that need to be done, and at least half of them need to be done right now. Jesus is telling us to prioritize. And when we prioritize, people always come first. So we look at the situation: overgrown grass, hungry kids, a concerned neighbor and a worried child. We know the grass can wait, and the kids won't starve. We go over to the neighbor or sit down with the child, and we listen.

When all is said and done, what does it matter if your house is immaculate and the beds are always made, or the garage is so clean you can see your face in the concrete? The bottom line is always about relationships. Jesus is telling us how important it is to take time from our busy schedules to spend time with him in prayer, yes, but also to take time to engage in attentive listening to those in need.

Family Response: As a family, practice attentive listening. Have someone talk about a problem he or she is having at work or school. Make sure no one interrupts until the one who is speaking has finished his or her story. Ask questions to better understand the situation. Suggest solutions only if the person asks for them.

Personal Response: Think of someone you know who is a good listener. What qualities make him or her that way? How good a listener are you? How can you be better?

_____

_____

_____

_____

_____

What do you want to remember from last week?

_____

_____

_____

_____

What are you looking forward to next week? What are your concerns?

_____

_____

_____

_____

Jesus' Teachings on Prayer

When Jesus' disciples ask him to teach them to pray, he gives them a prayer that speaks to the heart of our relationship with God. The Lord's Prayer is still the prayer of the Christian community. "Our Father, who art in heaven, hallowed be thy name…"

Notice how Jesus begins the prayer he gives to his disciples, "Our Father." The Aramaic word Jesus uses is *Abba,* which is actually closer to "Daddy." Read the psalms or the prayers of the prophets. Nowhere is God referred to as *Father,* let alone the intimate term *Dad.* Jesus is inaugurating a new relationship with the Almighty. It is no longer, "Majesty," or "the God of Abraham and Isaac." God is *our* loving papa.

> *Seventeenth Sunday in Ordinary Time*
> *Luke 11:1–13*
> *date: ___ / ___ / ___*
>
> **Our Father, who art in heaven, hallowed be thy name…**

Jesus is asking his disciples to change their image of God. And the change is dramatic. God is not just a creator; God is a parent. We are not just creatures; we are beloved children. But notice the pronoun before *Father.*

God is not just mine, but *Our* Father. God is parent to the entire world. Jesus is making the point that we are all brothers and sisters of the same God, the God we are to call Father.

Through Abraham, God made a covenant with the Jewish people. God would always be with them. They would be God's chosen people. In Jesus, God makes a new covenant, a closer, more intimate covenant. God is not just with us, but also in us. We are God's children. Jesus is our brother not just on his mother's side, sharing our humanity, but also on his Father's side, sharing his divinity. We are all one family. And we must treat each other that way.

Family Response: If your family is not already saying the Our Father together, begin doing so this week. Choose a time when the whole family is most likely to be together.

Personal Response: List the attributes a loving parent would have. Which of these qualities would you like most to possess? What can you do to make this happen?

_____

_____

_____

_____

_____

_____

_____

What do you want to remember from last week?

_____

_____

_____

_____

_____

_____

_____

What are you looking forward to next week? What are your concerns?

_____

_____

_____

_____

_____

A Parable About Greed

Jesus tells the crowd a parable about a rich man whose harvest was so abundant that he does not have room enough to store it in his barns. Rather than share his bounty, he decides to tear down his old buildings and build larger ones. "Be on your guard against all kinds of greed; for one's life does not consist in the abundance of possessions" (v. 15).

In this parable, Jesus isn't condemning the rich; he is telling us that if we have money, we need to use it wisely. When we have taken what we need, Jesus cautions us not to forget those who are in need. Jesus doesn't believe in stockpiling or building up a surplus. He has a much more global view of things.

Eighteenth Sunday in Ordinary Time
Luke 12:13–21
date: ___ / ___ / ___

Jesus is asking us to determine for ourselves just how much is enough. How many barns do we have to fill before we have enough? How many bank accounts? How many CDs, clothes or cars do we need? How big a house is big enough? Jesus is telling us it is spiritually prudent to share our abundance with those less fortunate.

"Be on your guard against all kinds of greed; for one's life does not consist in the abundance of possessions" (v. 15).

We are asked to trust in God's care rather than a surplus of grain or stocks or money. We are told that the world has enough resources to provide for all her inhabitants. Imagine a world where those resources were shared and everyone had enough, a world without greed. Imagine what it would be like if people were satisfied with what they have and did not covet other people's land or car or lifestyle.

This is the world God planned. This is the world of God's reign. This is the world we are all asked to work toward.

Family Response: Consider giving a family gift to some charity. Ask family members to decide what they can do to save the money and to whom it should be given.

Personal Response: What do you have a tendency to stockpile? Why do you think you have the need for so much? List three things you are willing to give away to a deserving charity.

_____

_____

_____

_____

_____

_____

_____

What do you want to remember from last week?

_____

_____

_____

_____

_____

_____

What are you looking forward to next week? What are your concerns?

_____

_____

_____

_____

_____

_____

Jesus Talks About Our True Treasure

Jesus tells his followers to be careful where they place their hearts, and how they prioritize their values. If they are given much, much will be expected of them. He goes on to warn them to be ready at all times to answer for their behavior. "For where your treasure is, there your heart will be also" (v. 34).

If asked where my treasure lies, without a doubt I would say my family. Probably my biggest regret is not having spent enough time with each of my children. Now that they are grown and busy with their own lives, I regret those lost moments.

Nineteenth Sunday in Ordinary Time
Luke 12:32–48
date: ___ / ___ / ___

> **"For where your treasure is, there your heart will be also" (v. 34).**

I learned the phrase *tempus fugit* in high school Latin class but never really understood its meaning until I reached middle age. Now I know how quickly "time flies." Toddlers become teenagers and, before you know it, you are celebrating a grandson's First Communion.

Time is a precious commodity, not anything to be squandered on "to do" lists. At its best, it is a gift that's meant to be generously shared with those we love. I remember the busyness of family life. It takes so much time to cook and clean, shop and do laundry, take care of the yard, attend Little League games, and on and on. There are only twenty-four hours in a day, eight of those spent at work or school, and of course we have to sleep.

It is so easy to let the days slip by with no time to play. But scientists tell us that play is an essential part of a healthy life, even for adults. Playing together as a family teaches us how to interact and develop relationships of trust and mutuality. We can learn to communicate in comfortable, informal settings. Play can even help us let go of aggressive tendencies. And it is a great way to relieve stress.

Try reclaiming Sunday as family day. After church, spend a few hours playing together. Fly a kite, toss a Frisbee or just sit home and play some board games. Sunday may seem the only day to get the laundry or shopping done, but try to rethink your weekly schedule. Spending Sunday with your family is a great way of keeping the Sabbath holy and honoring the Lord.

Family Response: Plan something fun to do for the whole family next Sunday. Ask everyone for suggestions.

Personal Response: What fun things do you like to do with your family? What keeps you from doing them?

_____

_____

_____

_____

_____

What do you want to remember from last week?

_____

_____

_____

What are you looking forward to next week? What are your concerns?

_____

_____

_____

_____

Jesus as Cause for Division

In this short excerpt from the Gospel of Luke, Jesus tells his disciples that he has come to bring fire to the earth. He will be a source of division in households: father against son, mother against daughter and so on. "From now on five in one household will be divided, three against two and two against three…" (v. 52).

Being a peacemaker is just part of the job description for parents. Squabbles over who gets the last cookie, who pushed whom first and whose turn it is on the computer are normal household occurrences. The secret to peace on the home front is finding solutions that strengthen relationships.

> *Twentienth Sunday in*
> *Ordinary Time*
> *Luke 12:49–53*
> date: ___ / ___ / ___
>
> **"From now on five in one household will be divided, three against two and two against three…" (v. 52).**

Peace is not the opposite of conflict. It is a way of solving disagreements without hurting each other physically or emotionally—and certainly without resorting to violence. In their book *Parenting for Peace and Justice,* Jim and Kathy McGinnis offer a four-step approach to bringing about peaceful solutions in volatile situations.

They tell us that unless children are threatening or engaging in abusive actions, it is best for parents to stay out of the argument. Children need to learn how to broker their own disagreements. When someone is hurting or threatening another, however, you need to step in and separate the youngsters. Send them to different spots to cool down and think over the situation.

After a little time, go to each child and listen (without comment) to his or her story. Bring the children together with the understanding that they will have a certain amount of time to solve the problem by themselves before you impose your own solution. The McGinnises report that because their solutions were almost always less tolerable than their children's, mutual solutions were usually found.

Learning to deal with conflict in a peaceful way is a valuable skill—certainly one the world needs. And by teaching our youngsters to be peacemakers, we are helping them realize their call to be children of God.

Family Response: Using each of the letters in the word *peace*, make a list of some things (words or phrases) that might bring peace to your family or the world.

Personal Response: What was the primary form of punishment in the family you grew up with? How do you respond to your children's disagreeable actions? What could you do to improve your response?

_____

_____

_____

_____

What do you want to remember from last week?

_____

_____

_____

What are you looking forward to next week? What are your concerns?

_____

_____

_____

_____

Jesus Talks About the First Being Last

When Jesus is asked if only a few people will be saved, he answers his questioners indirectly. He tells them that it will take more than familiarity with him or his teachings to get into the master's house, suggesting that they may be surprised to see who will be at God's table. "Indeed, some are last who will be first, and some are first who will be last" (v. 30).

Many of Jesus' sayings are hard. Surely this one, "the last will be first," is one of them. We live in a culture where success means being number one. Coming in last is unaccept-able. Yet, by his words and actions, Jesus teaches just the opposite.

Seeing the virtue in being last is difficult enough for us adults, but for a youngster, being last or left out can be traumatic. It can be wrenching to sit with a child who has been left out of a game or chosen last. I remember being barraged by all sorts of feelings—empathy, anger, frustration—when this happened in our household. It was hard to face the reality that I could not make the hurt go away.

So what can we do when our children encounter rejection? First, love them and listen to their pain. Allow them time to talk about the experience. Help them find words to express their feelings. Perhaps you can share a story from your own childhood about a time you felt rejected or left out. Later, you might read or tell them a relevant story from Scripture. For example, you could recall (or read from a

> **Twenty-first Sunday in Ordinary Time**
> **Luke 13:22–30**
> date: ___ / ___ / ___
>
> **"Indeed, some are last who will be first, and some are first who will be last" (v. 30).**

good child's Bible) the story of David, the last brother chosen who became Israel's greatest king. Or retell or read the story of Zacchaeus, who was disliked by everyone but chosen by Jesus to share a dinner.

When you share your stories and the stories of our faith family, you not only comfort your children but also plant seeds and provide a tool to help them grow. You are teaching them to connect their stories with the stories of others, and to discover that they are a part of a larger family where success and being first are measured with a different yardstick.

Family Response: After discussing how it feels to be left out, talk about people in your own circle (school, work, neighborhood) who might feel excluded. What can you do about it?

Personal Response: How do you deal with rejection? Do you get angry, cry, make excuses? Remember that even Jesus was rejected by his friends. How did he respond? How can you respond?

_____

_____

_____

_____

What do you want to remember from last week?

_____

_____

_____

_____

What are you looking forward to next week? What are your concerns?

_____

_____

_____

_____

Jesus Talks About the Virtue of Humility

Jesus warns his disciples not to feel too important. He tells them not to recline in the place of honor at a wedding feast. Rather, they should choose a lesser place and wait for the host to invite them to move up. "For all who exalt themselves will be humbled, and those who humble themselves will be exalted" (v. 11).

I took this reading to heart when I was young, and humbled myself whenever possible. My way of doing this was by putting myself down. It took my spiritual director years to straighten me out. I am still trying to learn that true humility is being honest about our gifts: not exaggerating them, not dismissing them and certainly not comparing them to others'.

It does God a disservice if we constantly belittle our gifts. I did that all the time. Someone would compliment me on my work, and I would respond by saying how much better Joan was at hers. It took me years to learn to respond with a simple, "Thank you."

Teaching children this kind of humility is an ongoing job. We often work so hard to help them grow in self-esteem that we forget to teach them how to internalize their real value and gifts. As a grandmother, I confess, this is one of my bad habits. My three-year-old grandchild can sneeze, and I'll start to applaud.

I remember reading somewhere that when a child gets to a certain age it's important to help her begin to critique her own

> **Twenty-second Sunday in Ordinary Time**
> **Luke 14:7–14**
> **date:** ___ / ___ / ___
>
> "For all who exalt themselves will be humbled, and those who humble themselves will be exalted" (v. 11).

work. Rather than gushing "that's great" for every dinosaur or flower she draws, a wise parent asks his or her child what the child thinks of her own drawing. Just make sure that the child doesn't equate herself with her work. Let her know that she is loved for who she is, not just what she can do.

Family Response: Ask family members to name two talents they have, and one talent they would like to have.

Personal Response: What are your gifts and talents? How do you use them to help yourself, your family and others?

_____

_____

_____

_____

_____

_____

_____

What do you want to remember from last week?

_____

_____

_____

_____

_____

_____

What are you looking forward to next week? What are your concerns?

_____

_____

_____

_____

_____

_____

God Is Number One

Jesus tells the crowds following him that being his disciple can be costly. They have to be ready to accept the crosses of their lives, and perhaps even the scorn of their closest friends and relatives. They have to be ready to give up everything, if necessary, to follow him and his teachings. "…[N]one of you can become my disciple if you do not give up all your possessions" (v. 33).

Jesus is not suggesting that having possessions is wrong or that we should give up everything we own. He is saying that nothing of this world should be valued more highly than our relationship with him and with those we love. I learned what this meant when my daughter was fourteen.

> **Twenty-third Sunday in Ordinary Time**
> **Luke 14:25–33**
> date: ___ / ___ / ___

> **"…[N]one of you can become my disciple if you do not give up all your possessions" (v. 33).**

One of my most precious possessions at that time was a beautiful porcelain statue from Spain that my husband had given me on a special anniversary. One day, while dusting the living room, my daughter dropped the statue and it broke. The scene that followed is indelibly recorded in my head. I went into a rage and my wonderful only daughter ended up literally backed into a corner. In a graced moment, the fear in her eyes got through to me, and I stopped yelling. I realized that nothing was worth hurting this precious child the way I was hurting her.

My initial reaction to the broken Lladro startled me. It was as though I valued that piece of porcelain more than my own child. I knew that wasn't true, but my response to its loss frightened me.

From that day on, I decided I would never own anything that I wasn't ready to let go of in the blink of an eye. My life has been a lot happier since then.

I know I'm entitled to own nice things (and I have some beautiful keepsakes in my home), but my things are not entitled to own me. How sad it is when our happiness depends on what we have or don't have. I think that is what Jesus meant when he said, "Happy are those who are poor in Spirit."

Family Response: Have everyone in the household name two things in the house that are most important to them (no more than two things, and people or pets don't count). You may be surprised at what they choose.

Personal Response: Are you attached to some things? What possession is most precious to you? Are brand names important when you shop? Why?

_____

_____

_____

_____

_____

What do you want to remember from last week?

_____

_____

_____

What are you looking forward to next week? What are your concerns?

_____

_____

_____

_____

The Story of the Prodigal Son

When the scribes and Pharisees chastise Jesus for associating with sinners, Jesus tells them a parable about a rich young man who takes his inheritance and squanders it. When he returns home to beg for mercy, his father greets him with love and forgiveness. Jesus is telling us about the unconditional love of God our Father. "But while he was still far off, his father saw him and was filled with compassion; he ran and put his arms around him and kissed him" (v. 20).

I know I affirmed my children when they were growing up, but I wish I had done it more often. In hindsight, I realize I got so caught up in the tremendous responsibilities of parenting that sometimes I missed what they needed most. Helping five youngsters grow up to be healthy—physically, emotionally and spiritually—is an awesome task. There were so many things to teach them and to protect them from. Too often, my conversations with them were not conversations at all; rather they were more like sermons with me preaching, teaching or warning against some danger or other.

> **Twenty-fourth Sunday in Ordinary Time**
> **Luke 15:1–32**
> **date: ___ / ___ / ___**
>
> **"But while he was still far off, his father saw him and was filled with compassion; he ran and put his arms around him and kissed him" (v. 20).**

One of the traits of a strong family is that its members affirm each other often. They congratulate one another on their achievements. They are quick to say "good job" or "well done." Even more important, they affirm each individual not just for what he or she does, but for who he or she is. It is our job as parents to model this love and affirmation, so our children learn to compliment each other and us, too.

We do this by offering gentle hugs and unequivocal compliments—words or actions that let our toddler or teen or young adult know they are loved no matter what. This does not mean we stop teaching or even preaching. It does mean we take care in what we say and how we say it. It also means we spend time each day listening to our children, affirming them and assuring them that they are loved. In short, we are asked to reflect God's unconditional love to our children.

Mirroring that love can be a difficult task if we do not first accept God's unconditional love for us. We need to remind ourselves that we, too, are God's children, loved with a love that is unearned and unending.

Family Response: Have family members write or draw one or two things they most like in each of the other family members. Show what you have each written or drawn.

Personal Response: Do you find it difficult to believe that God loves you unconditionally? Why or why not? How can you bring yourself to trust more deeply in God's love?

_____

_____

_____

_____

What do you want to remember from last week?

_____

_____

_____

What are you looking forward to next week? What are your concerns?

_____

_____

_____

Jesus Talks About Problem Solving
Jesus tells his disciples a parable about being wise and
trustworthy, telling them that if they cannot be trusted in small
matters they cannot be trusted in larger matters. Jesus concludes
by telling them they cannot serve two masters. "You cannot serve
God and wealth" (v. 13).

It is such a simple statement of truth, "We cannot serve both God
and money." No Christian of faith could possibly disagree. But if we
rephrase the question and ask, "How important is
money to you?" the issue gets a little cloudier.

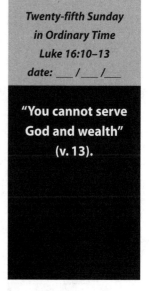

*Twenty-fifth Sunday
in Ordinary Time
Luke 16:10–13
date: ___ /___ /___*

**"You cannot serve
God and wealth"
(v. 13).**

Money is an important part of our lives. There
is no question that we need money to put food
on the family table, clothes on our bodies and a
roof over our heads. Earning money to provide
these things is definitely in the service of God.
Even providing luxuries for ourselves and our
families is okay, as long as we are also providing
for people in need. But when money becomes an
end in itself, buying becomes a way of life or
having this year's model becomes a necessity, we
are in trouble.

It is so easy to get caught up in the false
notion that things can make us happy, even
though we know that the pleasure they offer is temporary. Forever
happiness—day-into-the-dark-of-night happiness—is found in
God's love and in our relationships with family and friends.

Every once in a while it's important to check out our priorities,
and reevaluate our life style. There are at least two ways of doing

this: taking a good look around our homes and paying attention to what we find ourselves talking about. Both can tell us a great deal about what is important to us and who we are really serving.

Family Response: Talk about people you most admire. Why did you choose them? Is their worth dependent on the amount of money or the number of things they have?

Personal Response: What do you and your friends talk most about? What does this tell you about yourself?

_____

_____

_____

_____

_____

_____

_____

What do you want to remember from last week?

_____

_____

_____

_____

_____

_____

What are you looking forward to next week? What are your concerns?

_____

_____

_____

_____

_____

The Rich Man and Lazarus

Jesus warns us to pay attention to the poor. He tells a parable about a rich man who passes a beggar named Lazarus every day and gives him nothing. When both men die, the beggar goes to Abraham, and the rich man goes to his torment in the netherworld. Jesus is telling us to share the good things we have, and to give from our bounty. "And at his gate lay a poor man named Lazarus, covered with sores, who longed to satisfy his hunger with what fell from the rich man's table…" (vv. 20–21).

I learned about giving from one's bounty when my youngest son, Peter, was four. I was sorting through his T-shirts one day, putting aside some of the older and faded ones for the parish clothing drive. When he asked what I was doing, I told him they were for some poor children. He went to his bottom drawer and pulled out three relatively new shirts and brought them to me, telling me he was sure the children would like those better.

> *Twenty-sixth Sunday in Ordinary Time*
> *Luke 16:19–31*
> date: ___ / ___ / ___

> "And at his gate lay a poor man named Lazarus, covered with sores, who longed to satisfy his hunger with what fell from the rich man's table…" (vv. 20–21).

That afternoon, I realized the difference between Christian charity and simply donating to the poor. I began to understand that with true charity there are no "haves" and "have-nots." Christian charity involves a sharing of equals, who are all members of God's family. This subtle difference of attitude was made clear to me when my four-year-old just wanted to share with another little boy.

Why not make an effort as a family to give from your bounty?

Talk to your children about being a part of God's family. Ask them to choose some of their toys or other articles to share with brothers and sisters they may never meet. Model this spirit of giving by sharing some things that you still value. You might also choose to have a soup-and-crackers meal. By leaving the table still hungry, you can choose to experience a bit of the hunger many people have no chance to avoid.

True acts of Christian charity bridge the gap between the "haves" and the "have-nots." They are steps to building a world where everyone has enough. It's a great lesson for all of us to learn: sharing with our brothers and sisters and learning to give from our best rather than our surplus.

Family Response: Ask family members to think of one good deed they can do in the coming week. Share your ideas. Next week, remember to ask how each person did.

Personal Response: Parents practice acts of charity all the time. What acts of kindness have you done lately for your family or for an individual family member? Congratulate yourself for your unselfishness.

_____

_____

_____

What do you want to remember from last week?

_____

_____

_____

What are you looking forward to next week? What are your concerns?

_____

_____

_____

Faith the Size of a Mustard Seed

Jesus tells his apostles that if they have faith the size of a mustard seed, they will be able to uproot a mulberry tree and plant it in the sea. "The apostles said to the Lord, 'Increase our faith!'" (v. 5).

Some of the greatest theologians and saints once questioned the existence of God. It's not a sin to doubt our faith. Sometimes it's a healthy sign of growth. But it can be pretty scary when our youngsters begin questioning the truths we hold most sacred.

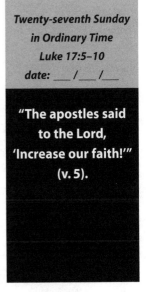

Twenty-seventh Sunday in Ordinary Time
Luke 17:5–10
date: ___ / ___ / ___

"The apostles said to the Lord, 'Increase our faith!'" (v. 5).

My youngest son was fourteen when he put the question to me: "Mom, what if there isn't a God?" After some discussion about what he was thinking and feeling, I realized he was just as concerned about the fact that he was questioning as the question itself. I offered some advice that I've tried to follow myself: "As long as you keep honestly searching for the truth, you'll be fine."

This search for truth can be a lifelong adventure; questioning and even doubting are often a part of the process. Our job as parents is to lay a solid faith foundation so our children feel free to ask their questions, but also know where to look for answers. We do this from their earliest years by sharing Scripture and praying with them, by talking about what we believe and by taking them to church to worship, learn and serve with their peers and the larger parish.

We cannot argue our children into faith. We cannot make them believe. We know they were gifted with faith at their baptism, and we can only trust that if they keep honestly searching for the truth, they will find it. In the end they will see God, because God is truth.

Family Response: Talk about the good deeds family members did last week. Ask each family member to think about the following question: "If you could ask God one question, what would it be?" Share your questions.

Personal Response: Is faith important to you? Why or why not? If it is important, in what ways do you model your faith at home?

_____

_____

_____

_____

_____

_____

_____

What do you want to remember from last week?

_____

_____

_____

_____

_____

_____

What are you looking forward to next week? What are your concerns?

_____

_____

_____

_____

_____

_____

Jesus Heals the Ten Lepers
Ten lepers ask Jesus for healing. Jesus tells them to show
themselves to the priest. As they leave Jesus, they realize they are
healed. Only one, a Samaritan, comes back to thank Jesus.
"Was none of them found to return and give praise to God
except this foreigner?" (v. 18).

What happened to those other nine lepers who were cured? Why
didn't they come back to thank Jesus? I've given it some thought,
and I have come up with nine reasonable
rationalizations. Some sounded pretty familiar to
my ears. You could probably come up with a few
of your own. Here are mine:

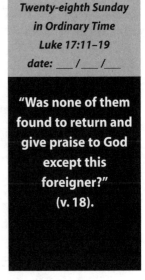

*Twenty-eighth Sunday
in Ordinary Time
Luke 17:11–19*
date: ___ / ___ / ___

**"Was none of them
found to return and
give praise to God
except this
foreigner?"
(v. 18).**

1. I want to get back to my family or friends
   or work. He'll understand.
2. I'll do it later. Maybe I'll even write him a
   nice note.
3. It probably wasn't even a miracle. Maybe I
   just had a bad case of psoriasis.
4. Such a great guy doesn't expect thanks.
5. I have to get to the priest and do the
   required ritual, or the miracle might not
   last.
6. I never did anything to deserve getting
   leprosy, so I deserve the cure.
7. Why say thanks? Miracles are this guy's business.
8. I don't have time to double back.
9. I asked one of the other lepers to say thanks for me.

Teach your children not just to say "thank you," but to plant their feet firmly on the ground, look the person in the eyes and say the words meaningfully. A person who is truly grateful is a person who understands the give and take of relationships. They are also more likely to begin to appreciate the everyday gifts that surround them.

Family Response: Ask each family member to think of at least three things they are grateful for this week. Share your lists and say a prayer of thanksgiving together.

Personal Response: Besides your family, what are you most thankful for? Who are the people in your life who deserve your thanks? Have you thanked them lately?

_____

_____

_____

_____

_____

_____

What do you want to remember from last week?

_____

_____

_____

_____

_____

What are you looking forward to next week? What are your concerns?

_____

_____

_____

_____

_____

Jesus Talks About Praying Always

Jesus tells his disciples a story about a persistent widow who hounds a judge until she receives a just decision. He suggests they be as constant in their prayers to God. Luke writes that Jesus urged his followers to "…[P]ray always and not to lose heart" (v. 1).

Prayer is much more than the rote words we learn when we are children, or even the spontaneous prayers from our hearts. Prayer is more than just talking to God. There are three ways of praying: vocal prayer (praying with words or actions), meditation (putting our own thoughts into our spiritual reading), and contemplation (sitting with God in silence). All three forms of prayer have been a part of our Christian tradition for centuries, but the prayer of silence is probably the one of which people are least aware.

> *Twenty-ninth Sunday*
> *in Ordinary Time*
> *Luke 18:1–8*
> *date: ___ / ___ / ___*
>
> **"…[P]ray always and not to lose heart" (v. 1).**

In the last twenty years or so, young people have forgotten what silence is. Those traditional times of quiet (taking a walk, riding a bike, playing outside) are gone. Youngsters are plugged into sound constantly. Even we adults can't seem to walk into a room or ride in the car without turning on a radio, a CD player or an iPod. Yet we know that God often speaks to us in the quiet. Remember Elijah on that mountaintop? It wasn't in the wind, fire or earthquake that he heard the Lord. It was in the silence (1 Kings 19:12).

There is a tradition of prayer in our church called *lectio divina* (holy reading) that includes practiced silence. It involves four steps:

reading (usually from Scripture), meditating (thinking about or placing yourself in the story), contemplation (sitting in silence with a word or passage) and prayer (telling God what the reading meant to you). Small groups and individuals practice this ancient prayer form in monasteries and homes.

It can be a great way to pray together as a family. Lifestyles change with every generation. There are losses and gains. This generation seems to have an ever-growing access to information and a dwindling amount of quiet time. Helping our children appreciate silence is giving them a gift they can use all their lives.

Family Response: Gather the family and read a story from Jesus' life. Meditate on the story by asking youngsters how they might feel if they were one of the people involved. (Make sure you talk about how you would have felt too.) Then sit together quietly for a minute. Finally, ask everyone to say a short prayer out loud.

Personal Response: What was your prayer life like when you were a youngster? What is your prayer life like today? Write a short prayer to God in the space that is left.

_____

_____

_____

_____

What do you want to remember from last week?

_____

_____

_____

What are you looking forward to next week? What are your concerns?

_____

_____

_____

The Pharisee and the Tax Collector at Prayer
Once again, Jesus reproves those who believe they are better than others. He tells them a story about a Pharisee whose prayer in the temple gives thanks that he is not like everyone else, especially the despised tax collector he sees praying in the back. Jesus declares that it is the tax collector who is justified in the eyes of God. "…[F]or all who exalt themselves will be humbled, but all who humble themselves will be exalted" (v. 14).

Tax collectors were considered cheats and frauds—Jewish turncoats who worked for the enemy. The Pharisees were well-respected people of learning who were called to keep the people true to their faith and heritage. In the parable of the Pharisee and the tax collector, the Pharisee looks at the tax collector at the back of the temple and thanks God he is not like him. Whenever I hear this reading, I think of the supposedly Christian proverb: "There, but for the grace of God, go I."

I have heard folks quote this phrase when they see someone who is homeless or destitute or storm-ravaged, as if it is God's lack of grace that caused their situation or problem. I have heard others use it when they hear about some convicted felon or murderer. They forget that they undoubtedly have also refused God's grace and failed in some areas of their own lives.

Only someone who can honestly confess no sin could say, "There, but for the grace of God, go I," without exemplifying the

> **Thirtieth Sunday in Ordinary Time**
> Luke 18:9–14
> date: ___ / ___ / ___
>
> "…[F]or all who exalt themselves will be humbled, but all who humble themselves will be exalted" (v. 14).

pride of the Pharisee. Quite frankly the only proverb truly worthy of a Christian when observing another person is: "There go I."

Christ is in each person I encounter, whatever his faith or lack of faith. Christ is in all creation both on this earth and in this universe. We are all brothers and sisters, all one with God in the family of God. It is only when we can truly see our connection, this oneness that is God's plan, that God's kingdom will come.

Family Response: Go through newspapers or magazines and cut out pictures of people's faces. Put together a collage for the refrigerator and title it, "We are all God's family."

Personal Response: What person or types of persons in our society do you find it difficult to accept? How can you overcome this lack of love?

_____

_____

_____

_____

_____

What do you want to remember from last week?

_____

_____

_____

_____

_____

What are you looking forward to next week? What are your concerns?

_____

_____

_____

_____

_____

Jesus Meets Zacchaeus

Zacchaeus is short in stature and disliked by the people because he is a tax collector. He climbs a tree so that he can better see Jesus. Jesus calls Zacchaeus down and tells him he will be having dinner with him that night in his house.

It is safe to assume that most people in the crowd would have loved to entertain Jesus in their homes, but Jesus chooses the tax collector who is disliked by all. Undoubtedly, the majority of the people who surround Jesus and Zacchaeus are really good people. So why does Jesus pick Zacchaeus?

Zacchaeus certainly catches Jesus' attention by climbing that tree. He is a person interested in finding out more about Jesus. Maybe it is the crowd's negative reaction when Jesus calls Zacchaeus down that spurs the invitation. Jesus looks at the crowd, and he looks at Zacchaeus and knows the poor fellow needs help.

Two things are clear from this story: God's invitation goes out to all of us, and receiving that invitation doesn't depend on our own worthiness or goodness. It doesn't matter if we are short or tall, great or mediocre. God sees us with the eyes of a loving father. He wants us to become all we are capable of becoming. He has chosen us and invites himself into our lives. It is up to us to clear the path and invite him in.

Zacchaeus's response is also important to note. He changes. Once a rich man who may have used dubious means to acquire his

> **Thirty-first Sunday in Ordinary Time**
> **Luke 19:1–10**
> date: ___ / ___ / ___

> "Zacchaeus, hurry and come down; for I must stay at your house today" (v. 5).

wealth, he offers to give half of his money to the poor. That is how it should be with us, too. We will know that God is truly living in our hearts when our concern is focused on others, and not just with taking care of ourselves.

Family Response: Ask family members to think of someone they know who might need some encouragement or a friendly hand. Talk about how they can help.

Personal Response: Have you ever felt like Zacchaeus, lost in the crowd and needing some attention? What can you do about it?

_____

_____

_____

_____

_____

_____

_____

What do you want to remember from last week?

_____

_____

_____

_____

_____

What are you looking forward to next week? What are your concerns?

_____

_____

_____

_____

_____

Jesus Is Questioned About the Resurrection

Jesus' enemies, the Sadducees, who do not believe in the
resurrection, ask Jesus a hypothetical question about a woman
who survived seven husbands. "At the Resurrection, whose wife will
that woman be?" Jesus tells them that the coming age will be very
different from the present one. "…[T]hose who are considered
worthy of a place in that age and in the resurrection from the
dead…are like angels and are children of God…" (vv. 35–36).

I remember telling one of my theology teachers that I was
looking forward to heaven so I could have all my questions
answered. (Was it really just a lone shooter who
killed President Kennedy?) My teacher
commented that perhaps being in heaven
meant not caring about having all the answers.
That led to another question, even more difficult
to answer: What is heaven like?

> **Thirty-second Sunday
> in Ordinary Time**
> Luke 20:27–38
> *date: ___ / ___ / ___*

No one knows what happens when we die,
but the children of God know it's going to be
great. Through, with and in Jesus we will also be
with and in God. After the Resurrection we know
that we will be whole in body, spirit and mind.
Imagine life without any kind of pain or struggle,
filled with love, joy and all that is good.

> **"…[T]hose who are
> considered worthy
> of a place in that age
> and in the
> resurrection from
> the dead…are like
> angels and are
> children of God…"
> (vv. 35–36).**

I remember how difficult it was when my
mother died. The emptiness I felt after her funeral
was devastating. I missed her so much. But over
the years I have grown into a new relationship with Mom. I
experience her presence often, and know that she loves me now as

she was never able to love me when she was alive. She can love me unconditionally, like God loves me, and that is a great comfort.

That is what I think heaven will be like: being with Mom, Dad and my sister, plus a host of other folks, being loved perfectly and being able to love perfectly, just as God loves. Who cares about mansions or streets of gold? What could top an eternity of that kind of love?

Family Response: Discuss what each family member's idea of heaven is like.

Personal Response: What are your own thoughts on an afterlife?

_____
_____
_____
_____
_____
_____

What do you want to remember from last week?

_____
_____
_____
_____
_____
_____

What are you looking forward to next week? What are your concerns?

_____
_____
_____
_____
_____
_____

Jesus Talks About the Trouble to Come

Jesus tells his followers about the calamities ahead: wars and insurrections, earthquakes and plagues. He tells them that they will be handed over by people they trust and they will suffer greatly. But he also assures them that if they listen to him and put their faith in him, they will be saved. "By your endurance you will gain your souls" (v. 19).

If only we could shelter our children from all of the calamities and tragedies of life! But we can't. Our primary job is to get them ready for the real world—and calamities and tragedies are part of it. Besides, bad things happen even to the very young. Friends move away, parents separate, family members or beloved pets die, and those are just some of the possible tragedies. For us parents there is a great temptation to say, "Don't cry. Everything will be all right." It sounds like a very Christian response, rooted in faith and hope. In truth, the "Everything will be all right" part is fine. It's the "Don't cry" that needs to go.

> **Thirty-third Sunday
> in Ordinary Time**
> *Luke 21:5–19*
> date: ___ / ___ / ___
>
> **"By your endurance you will gain your souls"**
> **(v. 19).**

Tears are cleansing. They are a gift of our human condition. They communicate our feelings, allow for the cohesive bond of compassion and open the door to healing. But sometimes tears get stifled. It takes faith and hope to trust that all will be well, just as it takes courage and humility to accept our own tears and those of others.

We parents often have almost a compulsive need to make things better, to solve problems, to fix things. And so we say things like, "Don't cry," or, "Look at it this way," when often what our children really need is just our quiet presence and our loving support. It helps, when we find a youngster in distress, to take a few moments for some quiet prayer of our own—to ask for the grace to experience and share God's comforting love.

If we take the time to suffer our children's pain with them, then perhaps later they will also be open to talking about and processing the experience. As parents, we need to allow our youngsters to show their grief, offering our comforting presence and gentle support as a testimony to our words, "Everything will be all right."

Family Response: Practice attentive listening again. Have someone talk about a problem he or she is having at work or school. Make sure no one interrupts until the speaker is done. Ask questions to better understand the situation. Suggest solutions—only if the person asks for them.

Personal Response: Try some spiritual reflection. Consider something difficult that happened to you last week. Think about the situation and consider what Jesus might have observed if he were present. How might he have reacted? Sit in silence for a few minutes. Write your response in the space below.

_____

_____

_____

_____

What do you want to remember from last week?

_____

_____

_____

What are you looking forward to next week? What are your concerns?

_____

_____

_____

LENT

Jesus Is Tempted in the Desert

The story of Jesus being tempted in the desert is familiar to Christians because it is read from the pulpit every year on the First Sunday of Lent. Jesus leaves the crowds to go into the desert to fast from food and to pray for forty days. At the end of this period, Jesus is tempted by the devil to use his power for self-gratification and personal gain.

Most folks will tell you it takes practice to say no to temptation. Consider Adam and Eve when they lived in paradise. They never had to practice saying no because they had everything they wanted. The first time they were tempted, they failed the test.

In this reading, we find Jesus in the desert tempted three times by the devil. He was physically weak, hungry and thirsty, and still he did not give in to temptation. He said no, not out of some superhuman power but from good old-fashioned willpower. Since Jesus is fully human, we can presume this was not his first encounter with temptation. Jesus had spent a lifetime building up his willpower by saying no to the easy way out, no to having fun at the expense of others, no to putting his needs or wants first.

First Sunday of Lent
Luke 4:1–13
date: ___ / ___ / ___

"When the devil had finished every test, he departed from him until an opportune time" (v. 13).

How can we practice saying no to temptation? One way is by flexing the muscle of self-denial. Self-denial, or what we used to call, "giving stuff up," has been a part of Christian discipleship since Jesus walked with the first apostles: "…[G]o, sell your possessions, and give the money to the poor…" (Matthew 19:21).

Lent may be the traditional time to practice self-denial, but it doesn't have to be the only time. You can practice saying no to your sweet tooth or the urge to buy one more thing on eBay. You can choose to drink water as your only beverage for a few days. You can even skip a couple of meals one day to experience what it feels like to go to bed hungry.

By practicing self-denial once in a while, we learn self-discipline, an important virtue for Christians. Often learning how to say no to small temptations can be very helpful when we find ourselves facing larger ones.

Family Response: Decide as a household on something you can give up for the next week: candy, soda, potato chips. Have water at meals, or try fasting between lunch and dinner. Take the money you save and give it to the poor.

Personal Response: Giving up potato chips or chocolate can take a great amount of willpower. Giving up complaining about your boss, work or mother-in-law can take even more. Who or what is your favorite topic of complaint? Write it down in the space below, and then see if you can get through the next two weeks without mentioning it to anyone else.

_____

_____

_____

What do you want to remember from last week?

_____

_____

_____

What are you looking forward to next week? What are your concerns?

_____

_____

_____

Jesus Takes His Friends to the Mountaintop
Jesus takes Peter, John and James to the top of a mountain to pray.
Jesus' appearance changes as he prays, and his face and clothing
reflect the glory of God. The apostles also notice that Jesus is
talking to two men, Moses and Elijah. Peter wants to build three
tents on the mountain to mark the experience. But after hearing
God's voice proclaim Jesus as God's Son, the apostles leave the
mountain and tell no one what they have seen or heard.

Like Peter, James and John, we, too, sometimes have mountaintop
experiences. It is easy to pray at those times—to praise God or just
sit in quiet meditation. In those brief, personal
encounters with the divine, our prayers can
become deeply private and powerful. However, as
this Scripture reminds us, we can't stay on the
mountain.

More common are our valley experiences
with prayer: times when we are plugged into
every distraction around us, and God feels an
eternity away. Spiritual masters tell us that those
prayers that seem empty and monotonous can
be even more valuable than a mountaintop
experience.

Those same masters remind us that while
alone time with God is valuable, often Christians
pray best together. Christians are not theists who
believe in a totally personal, one-on-one relationship with God. We
are a covenant people who believe that together we are the body
of Christ. We believe in the Incarnation—God is with us and in us.

Second Sunday of Lent
Luke 9:28–36
date: ___ / ___ / ___

**"Master, it is good
for us to be here; let
us make three
dwellings..."
(v. 33).**

We don't have to go to mountaintops or valleys to encounter God, because we find God all around us in everyone we meet.

We find God in other people, in our parish church and in our homes. This is why communal and family prayer is so important. Every Sunday, we gather to pray together with our parish family. And so it should be with our immediate family. Choose a prayer space in your home, and gather on a regular basis. You may be surprised to find how this not-so-quiet family time can provide transfiguring moments when a kitchen or living room can seem like a mountaintop.

Family Response: Plan some time each day when your family can pray together. Gather in the same place, light a candle, join hands, say a simple prayer like the Our Father and then let people add their own prayers.

Personal Response: Are you comfortable praying with others? With whom do you pray? How often?

_____

_____

_____

_____

What do you want to remember from last week?

_____

_____

_____

_____

What are you looking forward to next week? What are your concerns?

_____

_____

_____

_____

Jesus Encounters the Woman at the Well

It is midday and Jesus is thirsty. He stops at a well for a drink, and begins a conversation with the only person there, a Samaritan woman. She is an outcast of the nearby village who is forced to retrieve her daily water in the heat of the noonday sun. Jesus gives her a chance to change her life by offering her water that will quench her thirst forever. She counters his offer with a question: "Where do you get that living water?" (v. 11).

No element is mentioned more in the Bible than water. Water cleanses, nourishes, irrigates, creates and even destroys. But, most importantly, water is crucial for life to exist, and this fact is nowhere more evident than in the desert.

The Samaritan woman has come to the well for water to drink, cook and clean with. Jesus offers her water that will do much more. He offers her living water that will quench her thirst forever and become in her "a spring of water gushing up to eternal life" (v. 14). The woman is a sinner, ostracized from her village, and Jesus is offering her new life. She has suffered the pains of her old life, and, smart woman that she is, she gladly accepts Jesus' gift.

The not-so-secret secret, of course, is that Jesus *is* the living water. Meeting with Jesus, even for that short a time, changes the woman. The townspeople notice the changes, and when the woman tells them about Jesus they

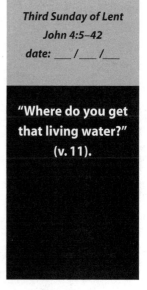

Third Sunday of Lent
John 4:5–42
date: ___ / ___ / ___

"Where do you get that living water?" (v. 11).

listen to her, and follow her back to the well. She has been healed, and now she, too, is able to share the living water with others.

The world is thirsty for the living water that Jesus offers. Where is Jesus, today, with his living water? Right here, in every local church and Christian home. All of us who have been blessed with this living water through baptism are called to share it just as the Samaritan woman at the well did. Like Jesus, we are to bring healing, forgiveness and wholeness to all those we meet. Like Jesus, we are the living water.

Family Response: Think about how your family or household can be the hands and feet of Christ and bring water to the thirsty. Where do you see people in practical or spiritual need? How can you be Christ in their midst?

Personal Response: Consider the people you work with, meet with or talk to on a regular basis. Are any of them in need of material, emotional or spiritual help? Can you offer to help them? Are you in need of material, emotional or spiritual help? Who can you go to for help?

_____

_____

_____

_____

What do you want to remember from last week?

_____

_____

What are you looking forward to next week? What are your concerns?

_____

_____

_____

Jesus Heals a Man Born Blind

Jesus refutes the misconception that physical handicaps are a punishment sent by God for a person's or the person's parents' sins. When Jesus and his disciples encounter a man born blind, Jesus heals the man and tells his disciples that the blindness was neither the fault of the man nor of his parents. When the healed man tells the Pharisees about the miracle, they refuse to listen to him because they still consider him a sinner. The blind man explains, "One thing I do know, that though I was blind, now I see" (v. 25).

When the Pharisees see the blind man who is healed, they do not see his open-eyed joy or excitement. They see a beggar, a sinner who sat outside the gates for as many years as they can remember.

Fourth Sunday of Lent
John 9:1–41
date: ___ / ___ /___

They hear his testimony, and the testimony of his parents, and presumably the testimony of the people who brought the man to them. But they don't really listen to what is being said. They still only see and hear a beggar, a sinner who is certainly not worthy of enlightening them.

"One thing I do know, that though I was blind, now I see" (v. 25).

By closing their eyes to the joy and wonder right in front of them, they miss out on seeing Jesus reflected in the eyes of the man once blind. By listening to only their own voices and the words they expect to hear from others, they fail to receive their own blessing, perhaps even their own salvation.

I wonder how often I do the same thing— react to what I see and pay little attention to what I hear. I see one of my children's friends and judge him on my first impression. I see milk spilled on the counter and the floor and do not really listen to the apology or explanation. It takes time to look beyond what we see—to see past our prejudice or anger or frustration. It takes time to really listen— to hear what is in someone's mind and heart. Yet if we don't take the time, we are like the Pharisees, and miss an opportunity to see Jesus reflected in the eyes of our children.

Family Response: Play a game of observation. Have one person close her eyes while someone else changes his appearance in some way. (Have one of the players take off his glasses, untuck his shirt or change his hairstyle). Take turns being the observer and the one being observed. Talk about how easy it is to miss seeing all the details around us.

Personal Response: Just about every one of us wears blinders, which limit the way we see certain things or people. We have subtle (or not-so-subtle) prejudices, usually inherited from the family that raised us. Carrying these prejudices around with us is not a sin. Prejudice is like anger. It is what you do (or do not do) with it that matters. What are the blinders you wear? What prejudices do you carry with you?

_____

_____

_____

What do you want to remember from last week?

_____

_____

_____

What are you looking forward to next week? What are your concerns?

_____

_____

_____

_____

Jesus Raises Lazarus From the Dead

Lazarus's sisters, Martha and Mary, send word to Jesus that their
brother is very ill. By the time Jesus reaches the home of his
friends, Lazarus is dead. Because of Martha and Mary's pleading
and faith, their brother is returned to life after being buried
for four days.

When Jesus raises Lazarus from the dead, we see an amazing
display of his power—a power that can conquer even death. Even
those disciples who had seen Jesus heal the blind
and lame must have been astonished by this act.
Sadly, the impact is not the same for many of us.
We've heard the stories so often we sometimes
take Jesus the miracle-worker for granted.

Fifth Sunday of Lent
John 11:1–45
date: ___ / ___ / ___

Our children can be even more blasé. They
are growing up in world of superheroes. Games
and cartoons like *Spider-Man, Yu-Gi-Oh* and *Teen
Titans* are their daily fare. Even if you limit their TV
viewing at home, they will still hear about it at
school or from friends.

**"Did I not tell you
that if you believed
you would see the
glory of God?"
(v. 40).**

We know that children younger than seven
have trouble distinguishing make-believe from
real life, but that shouldn't stop us from talking
about "just pretend." And as they grow older it's
even more important they hear us talk convincingly about Jesus
(the real powerhouse of good and conqueror of evil). They need to
see and hear how important Jesus is in our lives. If they aren't
positive that *we* believe in Jesus, they may just grow up thinking
God is one more make-believe superhero.

Family Response: Take turns naming the things about Jesus you like the most. See if anyone in the family can think of a story from Jesus' life that illustrates the things that you each mention.

Personal Response: Who was a hero of yours when you were growing up? What did you admire about him or her? What quality of Jesus would you most like to have as your own? Why do you need or want it? How can you acquire it?

_____

_____

_____

_____

_____

_____

_____

_____

What do you want to remember from last week?

_____

_____

_____

_____

_____

_____

What are you looking forward to next week? What are your concerns?

_____

_____

_____

_____

_____

_____

Jesus' Last Hours

Jesus, the miracle-worker, enters the capital city of Jerusalem with the crowds cheering and waving palms. A week later, after the Pharisees convince Pilate to convict Jesus of treason, the crowd cheers for his death. This reading includes Jesus' celebration of the Passover, and his gift of the Eucharist as well as his passion and his final words before his death: "Father, into your hands I commend my spirit" (23: 46).

Every Palm Sunday, I remember the years of being distracted by wiggling children and the shuffling feet of teenagers as the Passion was read. This story of Jesus' last twenty-four hours is a long reading.

It begins with Jesus getting ready to celebrate the Jewish feast of the Passover with his friends. The Jewish Passover is the celebration of Moses bringing the Jews out of Egypt to freedom. Within three days the world would be celebrating a new freedom.

Jesus sends his apostles to find a suitable place to celebrate the great feast. They meet in an upper room where Jesus has his last meal with his friends. At this meal, Jesus gives them (and us) the great gift of himself as he blesses the bread and wine.

After the meal, Jesus goes to pray in the garden, where he is arrested. He then appears before the chief priest and Pharisees and before the Roman official Pilate. At first Pilate orders that Jesus be scourged and beaten, but the crowd (the same crowd that only a week earlier hailed him with palms and cheers) protests: "Crucify him!" Pilate eventually

Palm Sunday
Luke 19:28–40;
22:14–23; 23:1–49
date: ___ / ___ / ___

"Father, into your hands I commend my spirit" (23: 46).

relents. Jesus, condemned to die, carries his own cross through the city to a hillside outside the gates. There he is nailed to the cross, and, after three hours, he dies. And, as prophesied, three days later Jesus rises from the dead. (The latter is not part of the Palm Sunday reading; rather we hear about this next week at Easter.)

In the short span of three days, Jesus brings about a new Passover. Like Moses of that first Passover, Jesus brings us out of slavery, the slavery of fear, greed and prejudice, to freedom. The Passion and death, along with the Resurrection, are the very heart of the gospel.

Family Response: Help your children recall the story of the Passion. Read it from a good children's Bible, or tell it in your own words. Put together your own Way of the Cross. As a family, choose six to ten events from the last days of Jesus' life. Draw a picture of each event and hang them all on the walls around your house. As you walk around to each picture, make up a prayer for each station.

Personal Response: Often our own problems or crosses are mirrored in the events of Jesus' Passion. (Jesus is rejected. He falls for the second time.) Choose one or two of the events of the Passion and, in the space below, write a brief prayer concerning them.

_____

_____

_____

What do you want to remember from last week?

_____

_____

_____

What are you looking forward to next week? What are your concerns?

_____

_____

_____

EASTER

Jesus Is Risen

There is no question that Jesus of Nazareth was crucified; his death is a matter of historical record. But it is what happened on the third day after his death that changed history forever. Jesus, our brother and savior, was raised from the dead.

On Easter we celebrate that God's love conquered death and that Jesus is forever alive in the world. We rejoice in our freedom from the slavery of sin and the bondage of fear and anger that can lead us to sin. We rejoice in our own new life in Christ. Easter is an alleluia day. It is the greatest, biggest, most important feast day in every Christian's life, and it should be celebrated every day by every Christian.

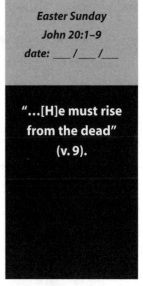

Easter Sunday
John 20:1–9
date: ___ / ___ / ___

"...[H]e must rise from the dead" (v. 9).

Jesus came to our tiny planet to help us remember something that we had forgotten: We are children of God. Jesus is our brother not only on his mother's side, but on his Father's side, too. He shared our humanity to remind us that through him we share in his divinity.

Jesus died for this truth, rose in this truth and lives in this truth today, through each of us.

In baptism, we choose to live our lives in Christ as lovers, healers and peacemakers. There is no place for greed or prejudice. And as we grow into the divinity Christ shares with us, we become more and more freed from the slavery of fear and anger, self-righteousness and false pride. We grow away from sin and become the person God created us to be, using our unique gifts and talents to make a better world.

If we remember who we are and whose we are, our everyday lives take on new meaning. If we believe that we truly share in Christ's life, then we know that nothing can defeat us. Does this mean we won't suffer or get hurt? Of course not, but we know that no matter what we encounter, God's strength and courage are at our disposal. We are not alone.

What a message of hope in a world full of all sorts of hurtful things. Share this message with your children, and celebrate your life in Christ. Celebrate Easter. Have a party!

Family Response: No matter what time of year it is, plan an Easter party. Work together to plan the party. You may even want to invite friends.

Personal Response: Easter is about new life. Where do you need new life in your everyday world? How can you claim it?

_____

_____

_____

_____

What do you want to remember from last week?

_____

_____

_____

_____

What are you looking forward to next week? What are your concerns?

_____

_____

_____

_____

Jesus Appears to the Disciples

After Jesus had been crucified, the disciples gathered behind locked doors, because they were afraid that they would be arrested as Jesus had been. But Jesus comes and stands with them. He shows them his pierced hands and feet so they know that it is really he who has returned. Twice he wishes them peace. He then breathes on them and tells them: "Receive the Holy Spirit. If you forgive the sins of any, they are forgiven them; if you retain the sins of any, they are retained" (v. 22–23).

When Jesus shows his disciples his hands and side, we are all given an important insight: The Risen Christ still carries the wounds of a broken world. In the glorified Christ we find all those who suffer, all those who are estranged and even all those who are unrepentant sinners. In this wounded Christ we find ourselves with all our own hurts and failings. What Jesus does after he presents himself to his followers is even more significant.

Second Sunday of Easter
John 20:19–31
date: ___ / ___ / ___

"Receive the Holy Spirit. If you forgive the sins of any, they are forgiven them; if you retain the sins of any, they are retained" (v. 22–23).

After he shows his disciples his wounds, Jesus breathes the Spirit into them. He sends them out as he was sent, to offer healing, forgiveness and, above all, love. This is our mission, too.

We are asked to love the beggar and the sinner as much as we love the self-reliant and the saint. The key is to remember that love is not just a feeling of attraction. It is a sense of attachment and acceptance. Love is a bond. It is realizing in heart and head that we are all one (sinners and saints) in the Risen Christ.

We can't help the way we feel, but we are certainly responsible for the way we act. We have to teach our children, through word and action, not to judge others so harshly that they fail to love them.

Family Response: Have a family reconciliation prayer service. Light a candle. Read the Scripture above just to the place where Jesus tells his disciples that the sins they have committed are forgiven. Ask each family member to think about a hurt they experienced from a family member that they are ready to let go of. When everyone is ready, ask each person to take a deep breath in and then slowly let the breath out as they forgive the person who hurt them. Close with an Our Father.

Personal Response: Are you able to forgive easily? What keeps you from letting go of old hurts or wounds? Write a short prayer asking God to help you let go of your anger and disappointment.

_____

_____

_____

_____

_____

What do you want to remember from last week?

_____

_____

_____

_____

What are you looking forward to next week? What are your concerns?

_____

_____

_____

_____

Jesus Appears to Disciples Who Are Fishing

The Risen Jesus calls to the disciples who are out fishing, just as he had called to them years before. That first time, Jesus invited them to follow him; this time he commissions Peter to leadership. Three times Jesus asks Peter if he loves him; three times Peter responds that Jesus knows he loves him; three times Jesus tells him to take care of the others: "…Feed my lambs. …Tend my sheep. … Feed my sheep" (vv. 15–17).

Jesus specifically calls on Peter to lead the early church. Jesus tells Peter that he is not only to watch over and protect those in his keeping, but also to nourish them and take care of their needs.

> **Third Sunday of Easter**
> **John 21:1–19**
> date: ___ / ___ / ___
>
> "…Feed my lambs.
> …Tend my sheep.
> …Feed my sheep."
> (vv. 15–17).

There is a great similarity between the family and the church. In fact, since early times, the family has been called the "domestic church." Both communities share similar visions and tasks. Family and church both have the responsibility of nurturing, supporting and challenging their members to grow to their full potential.

Both communities were founded in love, and both function best when they remember love is both their source and their sustenance. Both communities are called to be welcoming and reconciling. Church members are called to learn, pray, play, celebrate and serve together, and so are families.

Unfortunately because of the splintering of time and collisions of interests in our lives today (both adults and children) being a "family" is no longer a given. Too often we find households of youngsters and adults who share finances and a roof, but hardly a meal or conversation. In today's culture becoming a family often takes deliberate, intentional planning.

As a parent you are responsible for the members of your flock. It is up to you to protect and nourish them, and, somehow in your busy schedule, find time to be a family.

Family Response: Sit down together and give yourselves a report card on how well you are doing as a family. Give a grade to each of the following activities that, done together, are part of being family: learning, playing, praying, forgiving, celebrating and serving.

Personal Response: If you are like most adults today, your life is incredibly busy. If you are a single parent, the word *incredibly* does not begin to cover it. Aware of this dilemma, after looking at the family report card (above), what can you do to bring up one or two of your grades?

_____

_____

_____

_____

What do you want to remember from last week?

_____

_____

_____

What are you looking forward to next week? What are your concerns?

_____

_____

_____

_____

Jesus Declares His Union With the Father

In this short reading, Jesus talks about his commitment to those who follow him. They will have eternal life and never perish. No one can take them from Jesus because they rest in the Father's hands; they rest in Jesus' hands. Jesus explains that this is possible because, "The Father and I are one" (v. 30).

John's Gospel was the last Gospel written. It is probably the most theological Gospel because Jesus' disciples had more time to consider and discuss their experience of being with Jesus. It is in John's Gospel that we hear Jesus tell his disciples he will send the Spirit to do just that sort of discerning. John's Gospel speaks most often of unity among the Father, Son and Spirit.

Fourth Sunday of Easter
John 10:27–30
date: ___ / ___ / ___

"The Father and I are one" (v. 30).

Believing in a Triune God is the absolute bedrock of our Christian faith. God is one, but God is also three persons. It is, and will remain, a mystery as long as we are part of this finite world. Father, Son and Spirit are not sequential. There wasn't God the Father and Creator first, followed by Jesus the Son and finally, the Spirit. Jesus, the Spirit and the Father have been one from the beginning. "In the beginning was the Word, and the Word was with God, and the Word was God" (John 1:1).

When it comes to understanding God, we are all children. Our brains are limited to finite time and space, and God is beyond all that. Once in a while, we allow God to break through and we experience the awesomeness of the divine. This is where we discover clues to the mystery of God.

It is through God's self-revelation to a people who lived centuries before us that we see the mystery begin to unfold. They tell us about their experiences of God through stories and metaphors, through history, songs, poetry and letters. We call this library of God's self-revelation the Bible.

It is important to remember, however, that the ultimate and final revelation of our Triune God is Jesus. Always balance the other books of the Bible with the Gospels.

Family Response: Talk about what a mystery is, and remind each other that God will always be a mystery. Then name the things you *know* about God.

Personal Response: Read John 1:1–14, and ponder the mystery of our Triune God. Let go of your need to know everything, and trust that God is with you and in you. Sit quietly with certainty. Write about the experience.

_____

_____

_____

_____

_____

_____

What do you want to remember from last week?

_____

_____

_____

_____

What are you looking forward to next week? What are your concerns?

_____

_____

_____

_____

_____

Jesus Gives a New Commandment

Jesus tells his disciples that he will only be with them for a little while longer. He then gives them a new commandment: "…[L]ove one another. Just as I have loved you, you also should love one another. By this everyone will know that you are my disciples, if you have love for one another" (vv. 34–35).

Every time I read Paul's description of the love Jesus practiced and in turn expects his disciples to practice, I cringe. Paul writes, "Love is patient…it does not insist on its own way…" (1 Corinthians 13:4–5). Perhaps this is such a difficult notion to embrace because patience does not come easily to me. When I was raising my children, it seemed an impossible feat to maintain my patience.

> **Fifth Sunday of Easter**
> **John 13:31–33, 34–35**
> **date: ___ / ___ / ___**
>
> "…[L]ove one another. Just as I have loved you, you also should love one another."
> (v. 34)

I love my children, and I would give my life for them. But there were times when they were young that I was anything but patient and mild-tempered. At one point, I had a six-year-old, three little ones under the age of three and a husband who traveled.

There were days when the children teased each other, screamed and fought, and I joined right in, screaming even louder. I would go to bed hating myself, resolving to keep my cool the next day, but I'd get up in the morning and before noon I would lose my temper again. Finally, on a retreat, I learned that there were some things about ourselves that we just can't change through sheer willpower. No matter how much we want to, no matter how many times we try, we just can't do it.

So, as the retreat director had suggested, I turned it over to God. Every morning, I asked God for the patience I needed to get me to lunch. At lunch, I prayed to make it to dinner, at dinner, to bedtime. And it worked. After a few weeks I woke up to a different household. Because I was calmer, so were the kids. God's patient love became mine. I'd like to say the change was permanent, but it wasn't. I'd break the cycle and have to start praying hourly all over again. But I learned something very important through it all. I learned that the love Paul was talking about in 1 Corinthians is God's love, which is even more powerful than a mother's love. The good news is that this love is mine for the asking, and once I receive it I am free to share it with my children.

Family Response: Talk about how difficult it is to change old habits and how we sometimes need God's help. Suggest that each family member writes down one habit he or she would like help with. Say a prayer together and burn the pieces of paper as a sign of your turning it over to God.

Personal Response: What old habit or trait would you like to change about yourself? How have you tried to change? How can you work at change in the future?

_____

_____

_____

What do you want to remember from last week?

_____

_____

_____

What are you looking forward to next week? What are your concerns?

_____

_____

_____

Jesus Offers His Disciples Peace
Jesus promises his disciples to be with them and in them if
they love him and keep his word. He promises to send the Holy
Spirit, who will continue to teach them and remind them of what
Jesus told them. Finally, Jesus tells them not to be troubled or
afraid. He promises them his peace: "Peace I leave with you;
my peace I give to you" (v. 27).

There were so many times in my years of parenting when all I
wanted was a little peace. With seven of us in the house, it seemed
there was always someone wanting something or
arguing with somebody. As toddlers and teens,
my kids badgered and whined, poked and
pushed. Often I just wanted to say yes when no
was the right answer, or give in to the loudest
protester just for some peace and quiet.

Sixth Sunday of Easter
John 14:23–29
date: ___ / ___ / ___

**"Peace I leave
with you; my peace
I give to you"
(v. 27).**

   Real peace, the peace Jesus talks about, is
not the same as the peace which is the opposite
of war. Arguments can continue, battles can be
waged, people can disagree—but we can still
experience God's peace. God's peace is not
grounded in a particular condition or position. It
is grounded in love. God's peace is an inner calm,
a certainty that all will be well.
   While peace and quiet do not necessarily go
hand in hand, I discovered early in my parenting
that I needed a little quiet to remind myself that God is with me
and God is in me. I needed to set aside time each day when the
kids were safely settled (usually during their daily dose of *Sesame
Street*) to sit in quiet prayer. And I needed a yearly getaway
retreat to rest and to restore body and spirit.

If you are like me and find it difficult to remain calm and not answer every angry word with an even angrier retort, if it is hard for you to say, "No, you can't," and not dissolve when called the meanest mom or dad in the world—then perhaps you, too, need to find some quiet time for prayer, to let go of your burdens and injuries so that your hands are free to accept God's gift of peace. Once you accept it, and rest in that gift, you can share it with all those around you.

Family Response: Set some time aside for family quiet time—a half-hour or so for reading or working with puzzles. Make sure everyone is in the same room, but allow no talking.

Personal Response: Find some time to be alone. Set a timer for five minutes and sit quietly in a chair. Put your feet on the floor, arms relaxed on your lap. Become aware of your breathing in and out. Try to get rid of all thoughts. Say the name *Jesus* slowly and reverently over and over. When your time is up, write about the experience of the prayer of silence below.

_____

_____

_____

_____

What do you want to remember from last week?

_____

_____

_____

_____

What are you looking forward to next week? What are your concerns?

_____

_____

_____

_____

Jesus Prays for Unity

Jesus lifts his eyes to heaven and prays to his Father. He prays for his disciples and for all those who will believe in him. He prays that they may be one as he and his Father are one, and that they will know that he is with them and in them.

As parents, we know how important it is to put up a united front. Children learn at a very early age whom to go to when they want certain things. And sometime before early adolescence, they also learn the technique of "divide and conquer." It is important for parents not to let their guard down.

Seventh Sunday of Easter
John 17:20–26
date: ___ / ___ / ___

After a few years of being married (or perhaps working through shared custody), as parents you will know what issues you tend to disagree about. Don't let your child take advantage of this knowledge. As parents, make a pact that when conflicts concerning the welfare of the children come up, you will discuss them before making any final decisions. For example, if a child comes to you with a request after she has already asked her other parent, simply respond: "We (your parents) will talk about (the request), later and we'll get back to you with *our* decision." Whether children know it or not, they need to have parents who back each other up.

> "The glory that you have given me I have given them, so that they may be one, as we are one. I in them and you in me...so that the world may know that you have sent me and have loved them even as you have loved me" (vv. 22–23).

I learned from my own parents to always show respect for my husband. In all of my growing up years, I never heard my dad or mom speak one word against the other. And my siblings and I certainly were not allowed to speak disrespectfully to or about them.

We were never allowed to call my mother, *she*, or my dad, *he*. My dad (who was from Poland), told us that every language except English had a distinct pronoun to use when speaking to people we were to respect. So Mom was always Mom and Dad was Dad. It was a habit my sisters and I formed when we were young and keep to this day. It was something my husband and I tried to teach our own children.

Family Response: The average American family only eats two meals a week with all family members present. If this is the case in your household, make those meals special. Don't argue, preach or watch TV at the table. Spend at least thirty minutes together at the table talking about your day, and afterward share the cleanup responsibilities.

Personal Response: Make sure you show respect for your spouse outside of your home, too. Try to limit talking about your spouse's bad points with others. Think about how your parents respected each other when you were growing up. Has this influenced the way you speak about your spouse? Do you feel respected by your spouse?

_____
_____
_____

What do you want to remember from last week?

_____
_____
_____

What are you looking forward to next week? What are your concerns?

_____
_____
_____

The Disciples Receive the Holy Spirit
After Jesus ascended into heaven, the disciples and Mary were
gathered together, praying and talking about all that had
happened. Suddenly, a strong wind filled the house and there
appeared to be tongues of fire that rested on each of them. Mary
and the disciples then left the house and went out proclaiming the
Good News and people from all nationalities could understand
them, "All of them were filled with the Holy Spirit…" (v. 4).

We are a Pentecost people. Like the first disciples, we are gifted
with the Holy Spirit so that we can share our faith with others. This
is not always easy. Many of us were raised to
believe that religion is a private matter. It can be
difficult for us to talk about God or our faith. And
yet, faith sharing, especially in families, is crucial.

The Feast of Pentecost
Acts 2:1–11
date: ___ / ___ / ___

"All of them were filled with the Holy Spirit…" (v. 4).

We live in a culture that in many ways no
longer supports Judeo-Christian values. More
than ever, young people need to hear and see the
people most important to them talking about
and living the gospel message. If faith is going to
be real in their lives, they need to see that faith is
a reality in the lives of those closest to them.

Pentecost is the day the disciples were
empowered by the Holy Spirit to leave the safe
closure of the Upper Room, and share their faith
with a city of strangers. Why not take the risk this
week and share your faith with those closest to you?

Family Response: Read or retell the story of Pentecost to your family. Talk about how you would have felt if you were in the Upper Room, and invite other family members to do the same. Discuss the Holy Spirit in your life. How have you experienced the gifts of courage and understanding? When have you felt the Spirit's fruits of joy and peace?

Personal Response: In the space below write down why God and your faith are important to you. Record or comment on what other family members have said.

_____

_____

_____

_____

_____

_____

_____

What do you want to remember from last week?

_____

_____

_____

_____

_____

What are you looking forward to next week? What are your concerns?

_____

_____

_____

_____

_____

Jesus Talks About the Spirit

Jesus is about to leave his disciples. He tells them he has much more to teach them but they are not ready yet to hear it. He promises, "When the Spirit of truth comes, he will guide you into all the truth…" (v. 13).

The bedrock of our Christian faith rests on the mystery of the Trinity—our belief in a Triune God, one God in three persons. For years, I categorized to whom I prayed: praise to God, the Father; day-to-day help from my friend, Jesus; and on test days, prayers went directly to the Holy Spirit. There is no problem praying in this way. It just got confusing for me when I began to imagine each person in the Trinity as a sort of individual power beacon.

> *Holy Trinity Sunday*
> *John 16:12–15*
> *date: ___ / ___ / ___*

> **"When the Spirit of truth comes, he will guide you into all the truth…" (v. 13).**

Our human understanding is limited, so when we speak about God, we speak of three persons. But we know there is only one God. The Trinity is not like three signal towers sending out waves of power or grace. God's power is not static; it is dynamic. God is love, a dynamic love that is always in motion, always in relationship—Father, Son and Spirit.

The self-revealing mystery of God is like a whirlpool of love, spilling out into and through all of creation, returning in a whirlwind of love. It is in this overflowing, ever-returning circle of love that we find God's power and grace. When we get caught up in that whirlwind, we experience the Spirit of Truth, and begin to know God beyond words or definition. The mystery is not solved; we just get an inkling of our place in it.

Keep yourself open to the mystery of our self-revealing God and teach your children to be open, too. We live in an age of instant answers. Encourage your children to explore and discover the mysteries of this earth. But remind them that there are some mysteries that can only be revealed when you allow them to unfold.

Family Response: Make a list of all the names and titles you know that refer to Jesus and God. Ask each person to choose his or her favorite name.

Personal Response: What is your personal image of God? How has it changed over the years?

_____

_____

_____

_____

_____

_____

What do you want to remember from last week?

_____

_____

_____

_____

_____

What are you looking forward to next week? What are your concerns?

_____

_____

_____

_____

_____

_____

Feeding the Five Thousand

Great crowds of people were gathered to hear Jesus speak. They had followed him a great distance from the town. The apostles suggest that Jesus dismiss the crowd so they can find food in the surrounding farms and villages. Instead Jesus provides for the crowd by blessing five loaves and two fish, and sure enough, "[A]ll ate and were filled. What was left over was gathered up, twelve baskets of broken pieces" (v. 17).

The story of the feeding of the multitude is a Eucharist story. At Eucharist, we, too, gather to listen and be fed by Jesus. And like the people on that hilltop, we, too, are all satisfied.

The Eucharist was Jesus' lasting gift to his followers. It was his way of being present in a very concrete way throughout the ages. When we receive the host and drink from the cup, we know that Jesus is truly with us and in us. And as we watch our brothers and sisters receive from the same cup, we realize again that we are one: the body of Christ given up for the world. Take time to celebrate elements of the Eucharist at home.

The Eucharist is a meal. We remember the Last Supper, the breaking of the bread, the blessing of the wine. The time your family sits together at table is sacred, too. Say a prayer when you begin. Treat each other with the respect you would pay to Jesus.

The Eucharist is a sacrifice. At the preparation of the altar we respond, "May the Lord accept the sacrifice at your hands...".

> ***The Feast of the Eucharist***
> ***Luke 9:11b–17***
> *date: ___ / ___ /___*
>
> **"[A]ll ate and were filled. What was left over was gathered up, twelve baskets of broken pieces" (v. 17).**

Parents know about sacrifice—giving up sleep to comfort a restless child, wearing retread sneakers so a teen can have new soccer shoes. We are doing our children a disservice if we don't teach them to sacrifice, too. Children need to learn the discipline of choosing a greater good.

The Eucharist is a celebration of new life. We become a part of Christ's body, sharing in his Spirit. In Eucharistic Prayer III the priest says, "Grant that we…may…become one body, one spirit in Christ." You and your children experience your life in Christ's through the give-and-take of everyday family life. Help your children to also experience that life with the larger church family by becoming involved in parish activities.

The Eucharist is a family affair. We celebrate it with our parish family, and we live it day in and day out with our household family.

Family Response: *Eucharist* is a Greek word that means "thanksgiving." Talk about all the things you are thankful for as individuals and as a family.

Personal Response: What does the Eucharist mean to you? How can you help the Eucharist become more of a family affair?

_____

_____

_____

What do you want to remember from last week?

_____

_____

_____

What are you looking forward to next week? What are your concerns?

_____

_____

_____

God's Kingdom Come

The Feast of Christ the King is always celebrated on the last Sunday of the church's liturgical year. It is our way of saying "Amen" to the Scripture readings we have listened to throughout the year. In Cycle C, the reading from Luke talks about the inscription at the top of the cross on which Jesus was crucified. The soldiers had placed it there as a way of mocking Jesus: "'This is the King of the Jews'" (v. 38).

What, where and when is this kingdom in which Jesus Christ rules? Before Jesus even began preaching, John the Baptist announced that the kingdom of God was at hand. Jesus, himself, announced that the kingdom was upon us (Luke 11:20). But he also said that it was yet to come (Luke 22:30). How can we explain this paradox of time and place?

The Feast of Christ the King
Luke 23:35–43
date: ___ / ___ / ___

"'This is the King of the Jews'" (v. 38).

The not-so-simple fact is that the kingdom of God is not a set place, nor a particular time. The popular idea of heaven (an afterlife for the good), and the kingdom of God are not synonymous. The kingdom of God is whenever and wherever we find God present in action—good triumphing over evil.

When John the Baptist proclaimed the coming of the kingdom, he was announcing the coming of Jesus. As Jesus walked the earth, he was literally God in action. He confronted evil wherever he found it—prejudice, greed, selfishness, even sickness and death—and he won. Wherever, whenever Jesus was and is, we find the kingdom.

And whenever, wherever people continue to bring Christ's justice, forgiveness, healing and wholeness, we find the kingdom.

All of this, the cosmic battle between good and evil, and the victory won for us through the life, death and resurrection of Jesus is recorded for us in Scripture. It is the story of our faith, a story that is not finished yet. We believe the fullness of the kingdom is yet to come. Jesus promised that one day good would finally triumph, defeating evil forever. On that day we will enter the full reign of Christ as King.

Family Response: The kingdom of God begins in your home. Talk about ways you can let others know you love them without saying the words.

Personal Response: What have you learned most about yourself and your family over this year of journaling?

_____

_____

_____

_____

_____

What do you want to remember from last week?

_____

_____

_____

_____

_____

What are you looking forward to next week? What are your concerns?

_____

_____

_____

_____

• Extra Journal Space •

Feel free to use the following pages to continue any journal entries
for which you need more space.

_____

_____

_____

_____

_____

_____

_____

_____

_____

_____

_____

_____

_____

_____

_____

_____

_____

_____

_____

_____

_____

_____

_____

_____

_____

_____

_____

_____
_____
_____
_____
_____
_____
_____
_____
_____
_____
_____
_____
_____
_____
_____
_____
_____
_____
_____
_____
_____
_____
_____
_____
_____
_____
_____
_____
_____